DADD

RISM
RIES

lume 8

Friendship 101:
Helping Students Build Social Competence

Juliet E. Hart Barnett and Kelly J. Whalon, Editors

 Council for Exceptional Children

 **DADD**
Division on Autism and Developmental Disabilities

The voice and vision of special education

Council for Exceptional Children
2900 Crystal Drive, Suite 1000
Arlington, VA 22202-3557
www.cec.sped.org

Library of Congress Cataloging-in-Publication data

Hart Barnett, Juliet E.
    Friendship 101: Helping students build social competence. Prism Series Volume 8 /
    Ed. Juliet E. Hart Barnett and Kelly J. Whalon.
    p. cm.
    Includes biographical references.

ISBN 978-0-86586-490-0 (soft cover)
ISBN 978-0-86586-492-4 (eBook)

Cover and interior design by Tom Karabatakis

Printed in the United States of America by AGS.

First edition 10 9 8 7 6 5 4 3 2 1

Contents

About the Editors

Prism Series Vol. 8,
Friendship 101: Helping Students Build Social Competence

Juliet E. Hart Barnett
Associate Professor, Special Education
Mary Lou Fulton Teachers College
Arizona State University
P.O. Box 37100
Mail Code 3151
Phoenix, AZ 85069

Kelly J. Whalon
Assistant Professor, Special Education
College of Education
Florida State University
1114 W. Call Street
P.O. Box 3064450
Tallahassee, FL 32306-4450

DADD Prism Series Editor

Michael L. Wehmeyer
Professor, Special Education
School of Education
Kansas University
Joseph R. Pearson Hall, Room 521
1122 West Campus Road
Lawrence, KS 66045

About the Contributors

Juliet E. Hart Barnett
Associate Professor, Special Education
Mary Lou Fulton Teachers College
Arizona State University
P.O. Box 37100
Mail Code 3151
Phoenix, AZ 85069

Matthew E. Brock
Graduate Student
PMB 228, Peabody College
Vanderbilt University
230 Appleton Place
Nashville, TN 37203

L. Lynn Stansberry Brusnahan
Associate Professor, Autism Spectrum
Disorder Programming
University of St. Thomas
1000 LaSalle Avenue,
MOH 217
Minneapolis, MN 55403

Erik W. Carter
Associate Professor, Special Education
PMB 228, Peabody College
Vanderbilt University
Nashville, TN 37203

Maureen Conroy
Co-Director of the Center for Excellence in
Early Childhood Studies
Professor
School of Special Education, School
Psychology, and Early Childhood Studies
College of Education
University of Florida
P.O. Box 117050
Gainesville, FL 32611

Sharon deFur
Professor, Special Education
Department of Curriculum and Instruction
College of William & Mary
301 Monticello Avenue
Williamsburg, VA 23185

Monica E. Delano
Associate Professor, Special Education
College of Education and Human
Development
University of Louisville
2301 S. 3rd Street
Louisville, KY 40208

Mary Frances Hanline
Professor of Special Education
College of Education
Florida State University
1114 W. Call Street, 2209J STB
P.O. Box 3064450
Tallahassee, FL 32306-4450

Heartley B. Huber
Graduate Student
PMB 228, Peabody College
Vanderbilt University
230 Appleton Place
Nashville, TN 37203

Mari MacFarland
Doctoral Student
Department of Counseling, Educational
   Psychology and Special Education
College of Education
Michigan State University
620 Farm Lane
East Lansing, MI 48824

Jose Martinez
Doctoral Student
Special Education, School Psychology, and
   Early Childhood Studies
College of Education
University of Florida
P.O. Box 117050
Gainesville, FL 32611

Tara W. McLaughlin
Senior Lecturer in Early Years
Institute of Education
College of Humanities and Social Sciences
Massey University
Private Bag 11-222
Palmerston North, New Zealand
Collaborating Partner, Center for Excellence
   in Early Childhood Studies
University of Florida
Gainesville, FL 32611

Joshua Plavnick
Assistant Professor, Special Education
Department of Counseling, Educational
   Psychology and Special Education
College of Education
Michigan State University
620 Farm Lane
East Lansing, MI 48824

Jennifer Riggie Ottley
Postdoctoral Fellow
College of Education and Human Ecology
Crane Center for Early Childhood Research
   and Policy
The Ohio State University
175 E. Seventh Avenue
Columbus, OH 43201

Patricia A. Snyder
David Lawrence Jr. Endowed Chair in Early
   Childhood Studies
Director, Center for Excellence in Early
   Childhood Studies
Professor, School of Special Education,
   School Psychology, and Early Childhood
   Studies
College of Education
University of Florida
P.O. Box 117050
Gainesville, FL 32611

Liz Stone
J.B. Atkinson Academy for Excellence in
   Teaching and Learning
2811 Duncan Street
Louisville, KY 40212

Kristin Tarantino
Graduate Assistant, Annual Giving Programs
Graduate Student, Higher Education
The College of William and Mary
301 Monticello Avenue
Williamsburg, VA 23185

Jason Travers
Assistant Professor of Special Education
Department of Special Education
University of Kansas
JR Pearson Hall Rm 521
1122 W. Campus Rd
Lawrence, KS 66045

Terri Vandercook
Associate Professor, Chair
Department of Special Education and Gifted
    Education
University of St. Thomas
1000 LaSalle Avenue
MOH 441 | Opus Hall
Minneapolis, MN 55403

Kelly J. Whalon
Assistant Professor, Special Education
College of Education
Florida State University
1114 W. Call Street
P.O. Box 3064450
Tallahassee, FL 32306-4450

Peggy Schaefer Whitby
Assistant Professor, Special Education
College of Education and Health Professions
University of Arkansas
117 Peabody Hall
Fayetteville, AK 72701

Foreword

When asked to write the foreword to *Friendship 101*, edited by Juliet Hart Barnett and Kelly Whalon, I began to reflect on my own journey as a teacher and researcher in the field of developmental disabilities (DD) and autism spectrum disorder (ASD). My early experiences in an institutional setting in 1970 as a teacher of adolescent students with intellectual disability (ID) and ASD taught me many lessons about the importance of social skills. I developed a pilot work-study program that enabled these students to leave the institutional school during the day for on-the-job training (Zucker & Altman, 1973). Students were transported to a large office complex where they engaged in various housekeeping tasks. Students had no problem learning the tasks but performed unsatisfactorily due to inappropriate behavior carried over from the institution and lack of proper social skills in the non-school setting. Based on this experience, the program was modified to focus more on the social skills necessary for success in this business environment and less on the actual vocational tasks. We were able to use various modeling techniques to elevate appropriate social skills, which led to increased success for these students with ID and ASD (Prieto & Zucker, 1978; Zucker, 1978). The lesson learned was that social skills were just as important as task skills for our students to experience success. In reading and examining this collection, it is clear that outstanding progress has been made over the past 40 years in research and intervention in this area.

For all students, social communication skills are essential to establishing lasting friendships and relationships with others and enhancing quality of life outcomes. Children and youth with ASD and DD frequently experience serious difficulties with developing social communication skills and present many challenges to their teachers and families. They also experience lower levels of peer acceptance and fewer friendships (Rotheram-Fuller, Kasari, Chamberlain, & Locke, 2010). In fact, problems developing social competence skills tend to be inherent for these students and persist throughout the school years (Eaves & Ho, 2008; Guralnick, 2010). These challenges are compounded by the fact that children and youth with ASD and DD are often placed in the most segregated settings where their opportunities for social skills development are limited. However, we know that children and youth with ASD and DD can benefit from social skills intervention. Thus, fundamental for these students is an explicit, intentional focus on social competence utilizing practices supported in the literature throughout their K–12 careers.

Empirically based and practitioner-focused, Hart Barnett and Whalon's timely volume is geared toward supporting teachers with their implementation of the most effective and practical strategies on developing social competence, friendship making, and recreation and leisure skills among students with ASD and DD. *Friendship 101* includes succinct chapters written by experts in the fields of ASD and DD to address the unique social competency needs of children and youth spanning the ages of early childhood through adolescence. Because of the heterogeneity associated with ASD and DD, emphasis is placed on assessment for instructional planning as well as evidence-based strategies to support learners with a variety of cognitive, language, and social needs. Moreover, chapters highlight skills essential to building social competence (e.g., organizing and maintaining play, interpreting social situations, joining in activities with others, participating in and maintaining conversations; Conroy & Brown, 2002; Cook & Oliver, 2011). Each chapter also includes a research-based review of applicable literature, a focus on instructional strategies, as well as at least one vignette, instructional plan, or other supplemental material for readers to readily and feasibly implement the strategies in their own instructional context. Importantly, each chapter also provides helpful suggestions to promote generalization (e.g., teaching multiple peers, providing ongoing opportunities to practice targeted skills in multiple, natural contexts, and teaching self-monitoring).

One of the greatest strengths and contributions of this volume is its developmental approach. Although many volumes focus on a specific age or grade level, *Friendship 101* addresses the applicable social skills needs of students across the developmental period, with logical social targets that are suitable to children and adolescents according to their age level. For example, at the early childhood level, contributing authors focus on social skills in the context of play, whereas chapters geared toward elementary-age students stress the importance of teacher and peer-mediated strategies as children develop friendships and engage in interactions with their teachers and peers in both academic and social settings. As students move into early and late adolescence, the focus of the chapters progresses to assisting youth with developing peer networks; "hanging out" in recreation and leisure activities; and directing themselves successfully through the world of dating, sexuality, and relationships. Teachers working with students of all age and grade levels would be hard pressed to locate a more practical book to help them provide their students with ASD and DD with the requisite social skills to navigate the world of play, friendship, recreation, and interpersonal relationships.

Although the majority of content is focused on the implementation of social skills strategies in school-based settings, a chapter of the volume is also dedicated to assisting families and caregivers seeking to improve their children's social skills in home- and community-based settings. Parental participation has long been considered a crucial component of special education, particularly for students with ASD and DD. This chapter provides teachers with a guide for how to assist families in implementing caregiver strategies to teach their children social cognition skills, build friendships, and capitalize on natural community supports to enhance their child's quality of life.

Key stakeholders with interest in this well timed volume will no doubt include general and special education teachers and other key service providers of children and youth with ASD and DD. In addition, faculty preparing teachers to address the social skills needs of this population will also find the volume useful in their coursework and internship activities. The majority of states in the United States currently lack specific licensure requirements for teacher preparation in ASD (National Center on Teacher Quality, 2007), and many teachers correspondingly report feeling unprepared to meet the challenges of working with these students (Teffs & Whitbread, 2009). As such, this volume provides teacher educators with applicable, easy-to-understand information to prepare their future teachers of children with ASD and DD on how to use best practices to meet the social needs of their students. Last, researchers interested in enhancing the social skills of children and youth with DD will appreciate the review of current and validated research-based practices as they are applied in naturalistic contexts.

With an emphasis on explicit teaching, *Friendship 101* offers a constructive and practical guide for general and special educators striving to ensure that all of their students develop the social skills needed to be successful across school, home, and community contexts. The editors of and contributors to this volume empower teachers and caregivers to maximize the social potential of their students with ASD and DD by providing lists of resources where readers can access additional information, explaining what constitute effective strategies, and making explicit application of these practices to real-life case vignettes depicting authentic social and instructional scenarios. In so doing, these students can be guided to accomplish the full integration into our schools and communities that in decades past had been considered unlikely if not impossible.

Stanley H. Zucker
Arizona State University

References

Conroy, M. A., & Brown, W. H. (2002). Preschool children: Putting research into practice. In H. Goldstein, L. A. Kaczmarek, & K. M. English (Eds.), *Promoting social communication: Children with developmental disabilities from birth to adolescence* (pp. 27–55). Baltimore, MD: Brookes.

Cook, F., & Oliver, C. (2011). A review of defining and measuring sociability in children with intellectual disabilities. *Research in Developmental Disabilities, 32,* 11–24. http://dx.doi.org/10.1016/j.ridd.2010.09.021

Eaves, L. C., & Ho, H. H. (2008). Young adult outcomes of autism spectrum disorders. *Journal of Autism and Developmental Disorders, 38,* 739–747. http://dx.doi.org/10.1007/s10803-007-0441-x

Guralnick, M. J. (2010). Early intervention approaches to enhance the peer-related social competence of young children with developmental delays: A historical perspective. *Infants & Young Children, 23,* 73–83. http://dx.doi.org/10.1097/iyc.0b013e3181d22e14

National Center on Teacher Quality. (2007). *Special education teacher certification and licensure.* Retrieved from http://mb2.ecs.org/reports/Reporttq.aspx?id+1542&map=0

Prieto, A. G., & Zucker, S. H. (1978). Modeling effects with severely behaviorally disordered children. In R. B. Rutherford & A. G. Prieto (Eds.), *Severe behavior disorders of children and youth.* Reston, VA: Council for Children With Behavioral Disorders.

Rotheram-Fuller, E., Kasari, C., Chamberlain, B., & Locke, J. (2010). Grade related changes in the social inclusion of children with autism in general education classrooms. *Journal of Child Psychology and Psychiatry, 51,* 1227–1234. http://dx.doi.org/10.1177/0145445512442682

Teffs, E., & Whitbread, K. (2009). Level of preparation of general education teachers to include students with autism spectrum disorders. *Current Issues in Education, 12(10).* Retrieved from http://cie.asu.edu/ojs/index.php/cieatasu/rt/captureCite/172/4/CbeCitationPlugin

Zucker, S. H. (1978). Sensitivity of retarded children's classroom performance to social psychological influences. *Education and Training of the Mentally Retarded, 13,* 189–199.

Zucker, S. H., & Altman, R. (1973). An on the-job vocational training program for adolescent trainable retardates. *Training School Bulletin, 70,* 106–120.

Introduction

Understanding Social Competence and Its Importance
Juliet E. Hart Barnett and Kelly J. Whalon

Friendships constitute a significant social experience for children and youth and enable them to develop and practice fundamental pro-social behaviors, such as mutual caring, emotional support, empathy for others, and sharing (Bauminger & Shulman, 2003). Friendship can be defined as "a social relationship based on interactions that are reciprocal, stable, and serve the functions of intimacy, companionship, emotional support, and affection" (Freeman & Kasari, 1998, p. 343). Consequently, friendship requires basic elements of social competence such as effective communication, cooperation, the capacity to understand and reflect on another's perspective, emotional regulation, and strategies for problem solving (Asher, Parker, & Walker, 1996). *Social competence* refers to the ability to integrate cognitive, affective, and behavioral states to accomplish goals in social contexts; more simply, it is how well children and youth get along with peers and adults in order to establish successful relationships and realize social goals (Odom, McConnell, & Brown, 2008). Dynamic and developing over time through repeated interactions, social competence is often considered the result of effective social skills (McCabe & Altamura, 2011).

Most children and youth develop social competence as they naturally interact with others across a variety of school, familial, and community contexts. However, children and youth with developmental disabilities (DD; e.g., intellectual disability, ID; autism spectrum disorder, ASD) experience difficulty developing social competence skills (American Association on Intellectual and Developmental Disabilities, 2013; American Speech-Language-Hearing Association, 2006; Guralnick, 2010; Lord & Jones, 2012) that are essential to establishing lasting friendships and relationships with others as well as enhancing quality of life outcomes (Carter, Sisco, Chung, & Stanton-Chapman, 2010; Stichter & Conroy, 2006). Although the extent to which students with DD have trouble acquiring social skills varies (Abbeduto & Short-Meyerson, 2002; Cook & Oliver, 2011; Hart & Whalon, 2011), their interaction skills differ from their typically developing peers (Carter, Ornstein Davis, Klin, & Volkmar, 2005; Guralnick, Connor, Neville, & Hammond, 2006), and they often experience lower levels of peer acceptance and fewer friendships (Carter et al., 2005; Odom et al., 2006; Rotheram-Fuller, Kasari, Chamberlain, & Locke, 2010). For some subgroups of individuals with DD such as children and youth with ASD, problems developing social competence skills are inherent (National Research Council, 2001). These challenges related to social competence often continue throughout the school years (Carter et al., 2005; Eaves & Ho,

2008; Guralnick, 2010). As a result, social competence skills are important instructional goals for individuals with DD throughout their K–12 education (Stichter & Conroy, 2006).

Unfortunately, children and youth with DD have more limited opportunities to develop the social skills necessary for social competence (Carter & Hughes, 2007; Carter, Sisco, Brown, Brickham, & Al-Khabbaz, 2008; Gallagher et al., 2000). To develop social competence, children with ASD and DD need multiple opportunities to interact with typically developing peers (Guralnick, Neville, Hammond, & Conner, 2007) in a variety of contexts and settings (McCollum & Ostrosky, 2008). Yet children with ID and ASD are often placed in the most segregated settings (Hughes et al., 2011), and even when they have access to typically developing peers they generally engage in peer interactions infrequently (Carter et al., 2005; Guralnick et al., 2006).

The interconnectedness of friendship and social competence is complex. That is, lack of social communication or competence affects the ability of children with ASD and DD to engage with peers, which limits their ability to learn from these interactions (Guralnick et al., 2007; Wolfberg & Schuler, 1999). These limits on social learning may exist in part because of a lack of ongoing reciprocal interactions students with DD have with the same peers, and it is possible that socially interacting with the same typically developing peer regularly could provide the structure and predictability needed for greater learning to occur (Guralnick et al., 2007). Moreover, research suggests that children with DD can establish rewarding friendships (Freeman & Kasari, 1998).

Regrettably, social competence skills remain underaddressed in classroom settings (Hume, Bellini, & Pratt, 2005; Wong & Kasari, 2012). Although teachers report that a focus on friendship is important (Hollingsworth & Buysse, 2009), they also acknowledge feeling unprepared to address the social skills of children with disabilities or their typically developing peers (Pavri, 2004). This is concerning because social competence is linked to a number of current and future outcomes of individuals with DD, including cognitive development and academic achievement (Bukowski, Motzoi, & Meyer, 2009; Cook & Semmel, 1999; Hughes et al., 2011; Odom et al., 2006; Stichter & Conroy, 2006) as well as future employment (Carter, Austin, & Trainor, 2012). Moreover, there is an emerging evidence base that demonstrates children with ASD and DD can benefit from interventions that teach social skills necessary for social competence and provide opportunities for children and youth to utilize these skills in natural contexts (e.g., Carter et al., 2010; Hughes et al., 2012; McConnell, 2002; Reichow & Volkmar, 2010; Stichter, Randolph, Gage, & Schmidt, 2007). Therefore, fundamental to the educational curriculum for children with DD is an explicit, intentional focus on the promotion of social competence (Hunt & McDonnell, 2007) utilizing practices supported in the literature (Hart & Whalon, 2011).

The primary purpose of this volume of the Division on Autism and Developmental Disabilities' Prism Series is to support teachers in their efforts to address the social development of students with ASD and DD. The chapters in *Friendship 101* provide educators with an evidence-based and user-friendly guide to developing the social competence of their children and youth with ASD and DD that not only pertains to both general and special education teachers but extends to parents, caregivers, and other key service providers. In addition, faculty and teacher educators charged with preparing teacher candidates to address the social skills needs of children and youth with ASD and DD are a key audience as are researchers interested in investigating and enhancing the social skill development of such children and youth.

In this volume we view social competence from an ecological perspective. Specifically, we understand that social competence is influenced by within-child as well as environmental factors. Children are influenced by their immediate surroundings and the individuals who are there—including family, school, and peer network members—as well as by the relationships between these environments (e.g., home-school relationships), the broader community, and societal or cultural beliefs (See Bronfenbrenner, 1994). Children's experiences and expectations in these environments often differ, but what is learned in one context informs behavior in other contexts. Further, social competence has been linked to a number of internal and external factors, including cognition, emotional regulation, gender, communication skills, family and school influences (e.g., parent stress, family supports and resources, mother-child interactions, child-teacher relationships, peer acceptance in the classroom, family arrangement of play dates), cultural values and beliefs about social competence, and others (see Odom et al., 2008, for a review). This ecological perspective is interwoven throughout the book; together these chapters emphasize strategies to build social competence within and across school, home, and community contexts.

We also recognize that, because social competence is a developmental skill, expectations for social behavior change over time. In other words, socially competent behaviors of children and youth evolve from early childhood to adolescence, as do the strategies used to address these skills. Social expectations and corresponding instructional goals modify throughout the school years as social expectations become increasingly more demanding (Hughes et al., 2011; Rao, Beidel, & Murray, 2008) and goals shift from an emphasis on social communication skills in the early years to establishing and maintaining relationships in middle childhood and adolescence (Kaczmarek, 2002). As a result, social tasks become more cognitively complex as it becomes increasingly important to interpret and understand the perspectives of others and problem-solve social conflicts. Peer groups even change over time from friendships with same-sex peers to mixed-gender groups (Kaczmarek, 2002). Therefore, chapters in this volume begin in the early childhood years with a focus on play and conclude with forming and maintaining interpersonal relationships in adolescence.

About This Volume

Chapter contributors translate research-based practices in a straightforward and concisely written manner using numerous real-life student vignettes, case examples, strategies for direct application to classroom and community settings, and lists of resources for further application. Every section of this book has been written collaboratively by expert educators and researchers in the field of disability.

In Chapter 1, Maureen Conroy, Kelly Whalon, and Jose Martinez provide explicit, step-by-step recommendations for appropriately and holistically assessing the social competence of children and youth with ASD and DD while utilizing observation techniques in the school setting. These authors explain that although understanding the research on the social difficulties experienced by individuals with ASD and DD as well as what constitutes effective social interaction are important elements when determining intervention goals, the heterogeneity associated with ASD and DD makes this information alone insufficient to drive instruction. The eco-behavioral assessment process outlined in this chapter provides teachers and caregivers with assessment tools to determine (a) the presence, absence, and effectiveness of important social competence behaviors;

(b) in which contexts students with ASD and DD are more and less likely to engage in interactions with others; (c) the social demands required in these different contexts; and (d) the opportunities for interaction and natural supports available in these contexts.

In Chapter 2, Mary Frances Hanline and Jennifer Riggie Ottley emphasize the important role of play in the preschool years wherein skills essential for later academic and social success are acquired and honed. These authors offer teachers and families guidance in the implementation of evidence-based practices that facilitate play skills in natural environments, thereby contributing to students' overall social competence. Promoting play as it applies to adolescents is picked up in Chapter 8 wherein Sharon deFur, Juliet E. Hart Barnett, and Kristen Tarantino describe how to facilitate meaningful recreation and leisure activities for youth with DD and ASD. Unlike most typically developing peers, most youth with ASD or DD need more precise instruction in leisure education that generalizes to unstructured settings, or more structured support for organized recreation and leisure activities. Viewing recreation and leisure as mechanisms through which people improve their quality of life, socialize, and develop skills and competencies, these authors highlight how teachers can engage family, peers, and community partners in order to assist students in developing the social skills needed to successfully engage in recreation and leisure activities.

In Chapter 3, Joshua Plavnick and Mari MacFarland describe the critical role of peers in the development of social skills of students with ASD and DD in elementary schools. Recognizing the impracticality of teachers and other adults serving as the sole intervention agents for social skills instruction and the strong research evidence for the value of using peer models, the authors provide a guide for implementing peer-mediated learning strategies in school settings. They demonstrate how teachers can teach peers in the child's environment to be social skills instructors and how they can embed explicit instruction in social interaction during a child's day without compromising academics. Erik Carter, Heartley Huber, and Matthew Brock then extend the discussion on the role of peers in Chapter 7 as they address the social skills needs of students as they reach middle and high school with steps to promoting peer networks. These authors point out how peer relationships and networks are often elusive for students with ASD and DD and provide details for implementing peer support arrangements as an evidence-based approach for supporting students to participate academically and socially in middle and high school activities. Noting how current educator-delivered support models can unintentionally impede the development of strong social connections among students, they describe simple steps for launching and maintaining peer support networks to foster the types of social connections that can make school enjoyable and rewarding for young people.

Three chapters in the volume address the responsibilities of adults, teachers, and caregivers specifically. In Chapter 4, Monica Delano and Liz Stone describe how teacher-mediated or child-focused interventions play important roles in social skills programming. In the context of three different student vignettes within their chapter, the authors apply four research-based, teacher-mediated strategies that include joint attention training, adult-mediated prompting and reinforcement, video modeling, and social skills group training. Their chapter also illustrates how teachers can (a) apply these evidence-based strategies in their classroom settings, (b) monitor the response of children with ASD and DD, and (c) adjust instruction accordingly. Relatedly, Tara McLaughlin and Patricia Snyder explore a teacher-mediated approach known as *embedded instruction* in Chapter 5. Embedded instruction, they explain, targets essential learning goals of children with ASD and DD and occurs during natural events throughout the child's school day in contexts in which the child is likely to engage in that skill in the future. These authors describe the embedded instruction model and provide specific illustrations of how to employ this model to teach children with ASD and DD effective social communication skills. In Chapter 6, L. Lynn Stansberry-Brusnahan, Terri Vandercook, and Kelly J. Whalon demonstrate approaches to partnering with families, whose role is essential to the social development of children with ASD and DD as caregivers arrange social opportunities that can lead to friendships and greater peer networks.

The volume concludes with Chapter 9, in which Peggy Schaefer Whitby and Jason Travers tackle an often avoided topic facing youth with ASD and DD as they progress towards adulthood: interpersonal relationships and sexuality. Individuals with DD present unique needs regarding sexual education as they are at risk for being socially isolated and have fewer opportunities to interact with and learn from peers. Because these adolescents are often isolated from their same-age peers and their parents are reticent to discuss sensitive issues, they may lack opportunities to learn about their sexuality or to engage in typical, age-appropriate social activities such as dating. These authors emphasize how special educators, related personnel, and parents can collaborate to help students engage in social relationships meaningfully, and enable students to make decisions about their bodies, their values, and their sexual and reproductive health.

We thank the authors of this volume for their valuable and practical contributions and collaborations to ensure such a high-quality guide for educators and caregivers as they seek to increase opportunities for social interactions and facilitate the overall social competence of their students. Supporting students' emotional growth, affective perspective taking, and social problem solving are important instructional priorities for children and youth with ASD and DD. It is our hope that the compilation of topics in *Friendship 101* will assist readers in helping their students achieve the interpersonal success that stems from a sense of belonging, self-worth, and meaningful social relationships for the long term.

References

Abbeduto, L., & Short-Meyerson, K. (2002). Linguistic influences on social interaction. In H. Goldstein, L. A. Kaczmarek, & K. M. English (Eds.), *Promoting social communication: Children with developmental disabilities from birth to adolescence* (pp. 27–55). Baltimore, MD: Brookes.

American Association on Intellectual and Developmental Disabilities. (2013). *Definition of intellectual disability*. Retrieved from: http://aaidd.org/intellectual-disability/definition#. VB8YhiiTLrg

American Speech-Language-Hearing Association. (2006). *Roles and responsibilities of speech-language pathologists in diagnosis, assessment, and treatment of autism spectrum disorders across the life span* [Position statement]. Available from www.asha.org/policy.

Asher, S. R., Parker, J. G., & Walker, D. L. (1996). Distinguishing friendship from acceptance: Implications for intervention and assessment. In W. M. Bukowski, A. F. Newcomb, & W. W. Hartup (Eds.), *The company they keep: Friendships in childhood and adolescence* (pp. 346–405). Cambridge, England: Cambridge University Press.

Bauminger, N., & Shulman, C. (2003). The development and maintenance of friendship in high-functioning children with autism: Maternal perceptions. *Autism, 7*(1), 81–97. http://dx.doi.org/10.1177/1362361303007001007

Bronfenbrenner, U. (1994). Ecological models of human development. In *International encyclopedia of education* (Vol. 3, 2nd ed.; pp. 1643–1647). Oxford, England: Elseiver.

Bukowski, W. M., Motzoi, C., & Meyer, F. (2009). Friendship as process, function, and outcome. In K. H. Rubin, W. M. Bukowski, & B. Laursen (Eds.), *Handbook of peer interactions, relationships, and groups* (pp. 217–231). New York, NY: Guilford.

Carter, A. S., Ornstein Davis, N., Klin, A., & Volkmar, F. R. (2005). Social development in autism. In F. R. Volkmar, A. Klin, R. Paul, & D. J. Cohen (Eds.), *Handbook of autism and pervasive developmental disorders* (3rd ed., pp. 312–334). Hoboken, NJ: Wiley.

Carter, E. W., Austin, D., & Trainor, A. A. (2012). Predictors of post school employment outcomes for young adults with severe disabilities. *Journal of Disability Policy Studies, 23*(1), 50–63. http://dx.doi.org/10.1177/1044207311414680

Carter, E. W., & Hughes, C. (2007). Social interaction interventions: Promoting socially supportive environments and teaching new skills. In S. L. Odom, R. H. Horner, M. Snell, & J. Blacher (Eds.), *Handbook on developmental disabilities* (pp. 310–329). New York, NY: Guilford.

Carter, E. W., Sisco, L. G., Brown, L., Brickham, D., & Al-Khabbaz, Z. A. (2008). Peer interactions and academic engagement of youth with developmental disabilities in inclusive middle and high school classrooms. *American Journal on Mental Retardation, 113*, 479–494. http://dx.doi.org/10.1352/2008.113:479-494

Carter, E. W., Sisco, L. G., Chung, Y., & Stanton-Chapman, T. L. (2010). Peer interactions of students with intellectual disabilities and/or autism: A map of the intervention literature. *Research & Practice for Persons with Severe Disabilities, 35*, 63–79. http://dx.doi.org/10.2511/rpsd.35.3-4.63

Cook, B. G., & Semmel, M. I. (1999). Peer acceptance of included students with disabilities as a function of severity of disability and classroom composition. *The Journal of Special Education, 33*, 50–61. http://dx.doi.org/10.1016/j.ridd.2010.09.021

Cook, F., & Oliver, C. (2011). A review of defining and measuring sociability in children with intellectual disabilities. *Research in Developmental Disabilities, 32*, 11–24. http://dx.doi.org/10.1016/j.ridd.2010.09.021

Eaves, L. C., & Ho, H. H. (2008). Young adult outcomes of autism spectrum disorders. *Journal of Autism and Developmental Disorders, 38*, 739–747. http://dx.doi.org/10.1007/s10803-007-0441-x

Freeman, S. F. N., & Kasari, C. (1998). Friendships in children with developmental disabilities. *Early Education & Development, 9*, 341–355. http://dx.doi.org/10.1207/s15566935eed0904_2

Gallagher, P. A., Floyd, J. H., Stafford, A. M., Taber, T. A., Brozovic, S. A., & Alberto, P. A. (2000). Inclusion of students with moderate or severe disabilities in educational and community settings. *Education and Training in Mental Retardation and Developmental Disabilities, 35*, 135–147.

Guralnick, M. J. (2010). Early intervention approaches to enhance the peer-related social competence of young children with developmental delays: A historical perspective. *Infants & Young Children, 23*, 73–83. http://dx.doi.org/10.1097/iyc.0b013e3181d22e14

Guralnick, M. J., Connor, R. T., Neville, B., & Hammond, M. A. (2006). Promoting the peer-related social development of young children with mild developmental delays: Effectiveness of a comprehensive intervention. *American Journal of Mental Retardation, 111,* 336–356. http://dx.doi.org/10.1352/0895-8017(2006)111[336:ptpsdo]2.0.co;2

Guralnick, M. J., Neville, B., Hammond, M. A., & Connor, R. T. (2007). The friendships of young children with developmental delays: A longitudinal analysis. *Journal of Applied Developmental Psychology, 28,* 64–79. http://dx.doi.org/10.1016/j.appdev.2006.10.004

Hart, J. E., & Whalon, K. J. (2011). Creating social opportunities for students with autism spectrum disorder in inclusive settings. *Intervention in School and Clinic, 46*(5), 1–7. http://dx.doi.org/10.1177/1053451210395382

Hollingsworth, H. L., & Buysse, V. (2009). Establishing friendships in early childhood inclusive settings: What roles do parents and teachers play? *Journal of Early Intervention, 31*(4), 287–307. http://dx.doi.org/10.1177/1053815109352659

Hughes, C., Golas, M., Cosgriff, J., Brigham, N., Edwards, C., & Cashen, K. (2011). Effects of a social skills intervention among high school students with intellectual disabilities and autism and their general education peers. *Research & Practice for Persons with Severe Disabilities, 36,* 46–61. http://dx.doi.org/10.2511/rpsd.36.1-2.46

Hughes, C., Kaplan, L., Bernstein, R., Boykin, M., Reilly, C., Brigham, M., … Harvey, M. (2012). Increasing social interaction skills of secondary school students with autism and/or intellectual disability: A review of interventions. *Research and Practice for Persons with Severe Disabilities, 37,* 288–307. http://dx.doi.org/10.2511/027494813805327214

Hume, K., Bellini, S., & Pratt, C. (2005). The usage and perceived outcomes of early intervention and early childhood programs for young children with autism spectrum disorder. *Topics in Early Childhood Special Education, 25,* 195–207. http://dx.doi.org/10.1177/02711214050250040101

Hunt, P., & McDonnell, J. (2007). Inclusive education. In S. L. Odom, R. H. Horner, M. Snell, & J. Blacher (Eds.), *Handbook on developmental disabilities* (pp. 269–291). New York, NY: Guilford.

Kaczmarek, L. A. (2002). Assessment of social-communicative competence: An interdisciplinary model. In H. Goldstein, L. A. Kaczmarek, & K. M. English (Eds.), *Promoting social communication: Children with developmental disabilities from birth to adolescence* (pp. 27–55). Baltimore, MD: Brookes.

Lord, C., & Jones, R. M. (2012). Annual research review: Re-thinking the classification of autism spectrum disorders. *Journal of Child Psychology and Psychiatry, 53,* 490–509. http://dx.doi.org/10.1111/j.1469-7610.2012.02547.x

McCabe, P. C., & Altamura, M. (2011). Empirically valid strategies to improve social and emotional competence of preschool children. *Psychology in the Schools, 48,* 513–540.

McCollum, J. A., & Ostrosky, M. M. (2008). Family roles in young children's emerging peer-related social competence. In W. H. Brown, S. L. Odom, & S. R. McConnell (Eds.), *Social competence of young children: Risk, disability, & intervention* (pp. 31–61). Baltimore, MD: Brookes.

McConnell, S. R. (2002). Interventions to facilitate social interaction for young children with autism: Review of available research and recommendations for educational intervention and future research. *Journal of Autism and Developmental Disorders, 32,* 351–372.

National Research Council. (2001). *Educating children with autism*. Washington, DC: National Academy Press.

Odom, S. L., McConnell, S. R., & Brown, W. H. (2008). Social competence of young children: Conceptualization, assessment, and influences. In W. H. Brown, S. L. Odom, & S. R. McConnell (Eds.), *Social competence for young children: Risk, disability, and intervention* (pp. 3–29). Baltimore, MD: Brookes.

Odom, S. L., Zercher, C., Shouming, L., Marquart, J. M., Sandall, S., & Brown, W. H. (2006). Social acceptance and rejection of preschool children with disabilities: A mixed method analysis. *Journal of Educational Psychology, 98*, 807–823. http://dx.doi.org/10.1037/0022-0663.98.4.807

Pavri, S. (2004). General and special education teachers' preparation needs in providing social support: A needs assessment. *Teacher Education and Special Education, 27*, 433–443. http://dx.doi.org/10.177/088840640402700410

Rao, P., Beidel, D., & Murray, M. (2008) Social skills interventions for children with Asperger's syndrome or high functioning autism: A review and recommendations. *Journal of Autism and Developmental Disorders, 38*, 353–361.

Reichow, B., & Volkmar, F. R. (2010). Social skills interventions for individuals with autism: Evaluation for evidence-based practices within a best evidence synthesis framework. *Journal of Autism and Developmental Disorders, 40*, 149–166. http://dx.doi.org/10.1007/s10803-009-0842-0

Rotheram-Fuller, E., Kasari, C., Chamberlain, B., & Locke, J. (2010). Grade related changes in the social inclusion of children with autism in general education classrooms. *Journal of Child Psychology and Psychiatry, 51*, 1227–1234.

Stichter, J. P., & Conroy, M. A. (2006). *How to teach social skills and plan for peer social interactions*. Austin, TX: PRO-ED.

Stichter, J. P., Randolph, J., Gage, N., & Schmidt, C. (2007). A review of recommended practices in effective social competency programs for students with autism spectrum disorders. *Exceptionality, 15*, 219–232. http://dx.doi.org/10.1080/09362830701655758

Wolfberg, P. J., & Schuler, A. L. (1999). Fostering peer interaction, imaginative play and spontaneous language in children with autism. *Child Language Teaching and Therapy, 15*, 41–52. http://dx.doi.org/10.1191/026565999667036164

Wong, C., & Kasari, C. (2012). Play and joint attention of children with autism in the preschool special education classroom. *Journal of Autism and Developmental Disorders*. Advance online publication. http://dx.doi.org/10.1007/s10803-012-1467-2

Chapter 1

Assessing Social Competence: A Step-by-Step Approach
Maureen Conroy, Kelly J. Whalon, and Jose Martinez

Joseph, a student with autism spectrum disorder (ASD), attends a third-grade class at his local elementary school. Because Joseph does fairly well academically in school, he spends most of his time in this general education third-grade class, but he also receives some additional support from Ms. Coffey, a special education teacher. One of the areas that Joseph struggles with is social competence. Joseph often has difficulty reading social cues and engaging in social interactions with peers. When he does interact with his peers, the conversations are one-sided and peers often lose interest when Joseph fails to engage them in the conversation. Joseph wants to make friends, but lacks the appropriate social competence skills needed to interact successfully with his peers.

Riley is a 4-year old with significant developmental delays in the areas of communication, cognition, and social skills. In addition to receiving itinerant support through her local school district, she attends Ms. Rosie's class in a community early childhood program five mornings a week to help facilitate her social-communicative skills and assist her in making friends. Riley likes her classmates, but often prefers to spend time alone. At this time, Riley has limited communication skills and typically uses motor behaviors (e.g., touching or pointing), but is beginning to learn to use some simple signs to communicate her needs and wants.

For many teachers, including Ms. Coffey and Ms. Rosie, teaching social competence skills is a relatively new area of educational emphasis. Although Ms. Rosie has certification in early childhood education and received instruction on the importance of social development and play skills in young children, and Ms. Coffey is a certified special education teacher and received instruction in remedial education, neither teacher was taught how to facilitate social competence skills and individualize instruction for students with developmental disabilities (DD), such as Riley and Joseph. Fortunately, researchers have been making substantial gains in instructional techniques to help students with ASD or other DD learn the skills they need to become socially competent. This chapter highlights a step-by-step approach that teachers and other school staff can use to assess social competence skills for instructional purposes.

Introduction to Social Competence

Social competence, defined as the ability "to successfully and appropriately select and carry out interpersonal goals" (Guralnick, 1990, p. 4), is an important skill for success in life. Most children and youth acquire social competence as they naturally interact with others across a variety of situations at school and in their communities. However, for students with ASD or other DD, social competence does not always develop without explicit instruction (see Brown, Odom, & Conroy, 2001; Brown, Odom, & McConnell, 2008). Students, such as Joseph and Riley, often have difficulty engaging others in social situations, responding to social requests or bids from others, and participating in sustained, reciprocal social interactions (American Psychiatric Association, 2013; Lord & McGee, 2001). Their difficulty in acquiring and displaying the skills needed to be successful in social contexts is typically a result of their delays or deficits across several key developmental domains, including communication, social, behavioral, or cognitive skills (Brown & Conroy, 2002; 2012; Kaczmarek, 2002). For example, Riley's cognitive delay and her limited ability to use language and communication impact her ability to socially interact with her peers. On the other hand, Joseph's behavioral excesses (restricted interests) and his inability to interpret others' social cues impact his ability to engage in meaningful, sustained interactions with his peers. Both students present unique abilities and needs in the area of social competence, which makes using a generic instructional approach to social competence less effective for them. Similar to instruction in other skill areas in the field of special education, one size does not fit all. For students such as Joseph and Riley, instruction in the area of social competence needs to be individualized, which means beginning with an assessment of each student's strengths and needs and developing an individualized social competence instructional plan based on the results of the assessment.

Assessment-Based Social Competence Instruction

Social competence is a complex skill set that is influenced by a number of factors, including our own social competence abilities, the social competence abilities of those we interact with, and the social requirements of varying contexts (Brown & Conroy, 2002; Kaczmarek, 2002; McConnell, 2002; Odom, McConnell, & Brown, 2008). Thus, we recommend approaching the assessment of social competence skills by engaging in a multiphase and multistep approach beginning with standardized assessments to examine the individual's strengths and needs and then moving into ecological and functional assessments to gather information about factors that influence social opportunities, which can set the stage for social competence instruction (See Figure 1.1).

Figure 1.1
Assessment-Based Social Competence Instructional Process

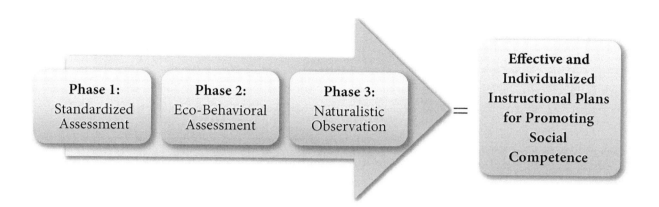

Phase 1: Standardized Assessments

Assessment of social competence for students with ASD or other DD should begin with a comprehensive evaluation of their strengths and needs across all developmental areas and domains: vision and hearing abilities; intellectual abilities; speech, language, and communication abilities; fine and gross motor skills; and social, emotional, and behavioral deficits and excesses. Because all of these developmental areas may influence the development and display of social skills, it is important to know in which areas the student may demonstrate deficits or delays. Typically, during this initial phase of assessment, standardized measures are used. In the area of social competence, several standardized assessments are available that provide a broad picture of how a student is performing in the area of social competence in comparison to similarly aged peers (See Cunningham, 2012; Sigafoos, Schlosser, Green, O'Reilly, & Lancioni, 2008).

Because social skills may vary across settings and situational learning activities, when gathering formal assessment information in the area of social competence McConnell (2002) recommends using multiple informants and tools to produce an authentic, representative, and accurate assessment of the student's social skills. Once the student's overall strengths and needs are assessed, we recommend using an eco-behavioral and functional approach to assessment to help improve how the student uses these capabilities within social situations and to help the teacher identify contextually situated social skill needs and opportunities.

Phase 2: Eco-Behavioral Assessment

Social skills vary depending on the types of social settings we encounter, and different social contexts require all of us to engage in different types of social skills. For example, in school settings, the social skills needed to be successful at lunch or during recess are quite different from the social skills required for success during a teacher lesson. Engaging in socially appropriate behaviors (that is, reading the social expectations and cues across these contexts) is an important part of developing social competence. For instance, Riley needs to know that when she is in a group play situation with her classmates, it is socially inappropriate to grab toys and other materials from her peers. Likewise, Joseph needs to be able to listen to and collaborate with his peers during cooperative learning activities without making irrelevant remarks or perseverating on his own interests. He also needs to learn to provide his peers with the opportunity to share their ideas and thoughts. Thus, using an eco-behavioral approach to social skill assessment can help teachers identify the most salient and context-specific skills to target for instruction and appropriate replacement social skills.

Once again, a multicomponent assessment that includes directly observing social skills in naturally occurring social interactions is recommended (Guralnick, 2010; Kaczmarek, 2002; Murdock, Cost, & Tieso, 2007). We suggest using the following steps as part of the eco-behavioral assessment to assist in gathering all essential assessment data needed for designing an individualized social competence instructional plan.

Step 1: Identifying contexts that provide social opportunities. To increase the likelihood for success of interventions aimed at increasing social competence of students with ASD or other DD, it is necessary to identify contexts that provide these students opportunities to interact with socially competent peers. A good place to start is by interviewing teachers or caregivers about situations and activities that can be targeted for instruction of social competence and which of these activities are enjoyable for the student. For example, if Riley enjoys playing at the water table, she will be more likely to engage in appropriate social behaviors with peers during water play as opposed to when she is engaging in a nonpreferred activity, such as finger painting. Because there is a strong academic focus in school settings, there are limited times when students are provided structured social opportunities during the school day. However, given the importance of social competence, it is important for practitioners to explore all opportunities that may exist for students to interact with their peers. For example, Joseph's teacher may want to target social skills instruction right before the school day starts, at lunch or recess, or embedded within cooperative learning groups during an academic lesson. In other words, students interact with others, including their peers, throughout the school day; thus, teachers and school staff need to identify opportunities that can help set the stage for learning social competence skills.

Step 2: Identifying social materials. Researchers have found that identifying preferences of materials to include in social opportunities can help when designing effective interventions (Boyd, Conroy, Mancil, Nakao, & Alter, 2007). In addition to identifying times or activities throughout the day that set the context for teaching social competence skills, it is also important to identify materials or topics of conversation that increase the likelihood of appropriate social interactions. Students with ASD, such as Joseph, can become preoccupied with a specific object or want to discuss a particular topic for long periods of time, which may interfere with peer interactions. However, with some students, embedding preferred materials within the social activity is more likely to increase interactions with peers. Thus, we recommend that teachers or school staff identify materials that can be incorporated into social competence instruction and are likely to increase the student's engagement in social interactions (rather than interfere with them). Interviewing the teacher or other school staff about students' preferences may help to identify these materials, or the teacher may want to conduct a more systematic preference assessment (see Boyd et al., 2007; Magnum, Fredrick, Pabico, & Roane, 2012).

Step 3: Identifying socially competent partners. In addition to identifying contexts and activities that promote social opportunities and interactions, it is important to identify social partners for students with ASD or other DD. Once again, identifying and including socially competent peers within social activities will increase the likelihood of students with ASD or other DD appropriately engaging in social behaviors during the targeted instructional times. Researchers have found that specific peer characteristics, such as the same gender, similar age, familiarity, and possessing the cognitive and social abilities required for social competence, are likely to increase the chances of students with ASD or other DD engaging in appropriate social behaviors (e.g., see Buysse, 1993; Guralnick, Neville, Hammond, & Connor, 2007; Hartup & Moore, 1990). In addition to possessing favorable characteristics, social partners should be motivated to interact with students with ASD or other DD. Increased effort on the part of the peers to interact socially with students with ASD or other DD increases the likelihood of the social interactions, which in turn increases the effectiveness of the interventions (e.g., English, Goldstein, Shafer, & Kaczmarek, 1997; Kohler, Greteman, Raschke, & Highnam, 2007).

Step 4: Identify critical context-specific social competence skills. Remember, social competence skills come in all forms and serve multiple purposes. For example, a nod or a smile acknowledges another person in the same manner as saying "hello." Working together on a puzzle or sharing the same art materials without talking to one another is also a form of social interaction in addition to sustained conversations with others. Many times, the type of activity and the social rules of that activity govern the type of socially appropriate behaviors. To identify critical social competence skills for a particular activity, we recommend directly observing the activity and identifying the skills that socially competent peers display.

For example, Ms. Coffey thinks that Joseph may initiate more often than his peers, so she watches the social behaviors of other students to determine how often they initiate in different settings and contexts. Peers can also be helpful in developing the intervention (e.g., Delano & Snell, 2006; Gena, 2006). If Ms. Rosie wants to teach Riley to initiate, peers are a great source for knowing how to join in or approach each other. By watching peers, Ms. Rosie can identify individually age-appropriate social skills to target for instruction so that Riley can effectively join in or invite peers to play.

Phase 3: Using Naturalistic Observation to Identify Instructional Targets

Because social competence is demonstrated naturally through interactions between students and their same-age peers (Odom et al., 2008), observation serves as the most direct method of assessment to help inform instructional planning (Guralnick, 2010; Kaczmarek, 2002). As mentioned, developing social competence can be difficult for students with ASD or other DD because social competence is influenced by a number of elements, including the social situation, skills of others, and characteristics of the student (Kaczmarek, 2002). Fortunately, school settings provide an optimal venue for observing students' social competence skills, as there are a number of meaningful social contexts throughout a typical school day that provide opportunities for learning social skills (e.g., arriving, departing, recess, lunch). Once again, observation of the target student's social skills can be most effectively implemented using a step-by-step approach.

Step 1: Observe and compare student's social competence skills. Ms. Coffey and Ms. Rosie plan to use observation to assess Joseph and Riley's current social skill strengths and needs during the school day. Ms. Coffey is concerned because Joseph is not well received by his peers, and a couple of peers have even begun actively avoiding Joseph. Ms. Coffey is hoping that she can identify instructional targets for helping both Joseph and his peers to build new and repair existing relationships.

Ms. Rosie will use direct observation to help her gain a better understanding of Riley's social interaction skills. Because Riley is withdrawn during play and has limited verbal language abilities, Ms. Rosie is unsure how often Riley is initiating toward her peers. She has seen Riley playing near peers, but other than grabbing materials, she can't remember the last time she saw Riley initiate. Ms. Rosie feels that Riley is getting more and more isolated from her peer group and would like to see Riley involve peers in her play more often.

Based on an interdisciplinary review of social competence, Kaczmarek (2002) presents three levels of social competence that begin with (1) specific, isolated skills necessary to engage in social interactions (e.g., greetings, initiations, responses) that when successfully applied in combination can result in (2) interactive, reciprocal communication (e.g., topic maintenance, engaged time interacting) that achieves a social goal. When children and youth are able to effectively socially interact with others, these interactions facilitate (3) peer acceptance and ultimately friendships. It is also important to observe if students display any problematic behaviors that may interfere with social interactions. Therefore, the frequency and quality of social initiations, responses, and interactions are often observation targets (Odom et al., 2008) as well as problem behaviors.

When conducting naturalistic observation in particular contexts, instructors will want to determine how the student's social skills match up to the social skills required for success (i.e., those skills previously identified through the eco-behavioral assessment). For example, when comparing Riley at the water station to her peers, Ms. Rosie found that Riley did not initiate with peers or share toys with others and unintentionally splashed other children when she got excited. To increase her peer-related social competence skills, Riley needs to learn how to initiate with her peers, respond to her peers' initiations, share toys with her peers for an extended period of time, and apologize if she accidently splashes others during her play.

Many researchers have developed coding systems to observe social effectiveness (Kaczmarek, 2002). For example, available coding schemes include various types of initiations (e.g., gaining attention, imitating, commenting, asking questions, making requests, sharing, offering suggestions), responses (e.g., contingent responses, imitating and following a peer), and interactions (e.g., initiation and response sequence, duration of interaction). In addition, coding schemes often address whether or not evidence of a target social skill (e.g., initiations to peers) is appropriate (e.g., asking a peer to play) or inappropriate (e.g., grabbing a toy away from a peer). Also, some coding systems define inappropriate behaviors that can result in negative peer interactions (e.g., inappropriate topic changes, competing with peers, ignoring peers, aggression) and identify the maintaining consequences (e.g., Conroy, Boyd, Asmus, & Madera, 2007; Conroy & Brown, 2002; Stichter & Conroy, 2006. Coding schemes using similar behavior combinations (i.e., initiations, responses, interactions) have been developed for use with young children (e.g., Boyd, Conroy, Asmus, & McKenney, 2011; Brown, Odom, & Holcombe, 1996; Guralnick & Groom, 1987), school-age children (e.g., Murdock et al., 2007; Theimann & Goldstein, 2001), and adolescents (e.g., Chung & Carter, 2013; Cutts & Sigafoos, 2001).

To help assess Joseph and Riley's social interactions skills, Ms. Coffey and Ms. Rosie each have decided to observe three target behaviors for their respective students and developed individualized operational definitions (see Table 1.1). As you can see, these include both appropriate social skills as well as behaviors that may interfere with social skill development.

Table 1.1
Examples of Social Competence Target Behaviors

Target behavior	Example
Initiations	Joseph makes a verbal comment or request directed toward a peer to get a response. An initiation is counted as inappropriate if it is an abrupt change in topic or is inconsistent with the topic. Riley makes a gesture toward a peer to gain attention, join in an activity, share an item, or get a response.
Responses	Appropriate Response: Joseph verbally responds to a peer initiation and the response is related to the topic. Inappropriate response: Joseph verbally responds to a peer but deviates from the topic or ignores a peer initiation. Positive response: Riley uses a gesture (e.g., nods her head) to respond immediately after a peer initiation acknowledging the peer initiation. No response: Riley does not respond to or ignores a peer initiation.
Interactions	Joseph is engaged in a conversation with two or more peers by contributing or attending to the topic.
Engagement	Riley is actively participating in play with peers (e.g., sharing toys).

Observing all instances of a behavior (i.e., event recording) can be challenging for teachers in a classroom context, which is why sampling methods are also recommended. Partial interval recording is a commonly used sampling method, and involves setting an interval (5–10 s) and documenting if the target behavior occurred at all during that interval. Figure 1.2 is a sample of Ms. Coffey's partial interval (10-s intervals) coding sheet taken during a 10-min recess observation Ms. Coffey uses the same recording method when she observes Joseph at lunch, waiting for the bus, and in his cooperative learning group.

Figure 1.2
Sample Coding During Joseph's Recess

Target behavior	10-s intervals																			
Intervals	1	2	3	4	5	6	7	8	9	10	11	12	13	14	15	16	17	18	19	20
Initiations	−	−	+	−	+	0	0	+	−	0	+ −	+ −	−	−	+	+	−	+	+ −	−
Responses	−	+	−	+	+	+	+	0	0	0	0	0	0	+	+	−	0	0	−	+
Interactions	0	0	0	0	0	0	0	0	0	1	0	0	0	0	0	0	1	0	0	0

Initiations and responses: Record a + if an appropriate initiation or response occurred in an interval, a − if an inappropriate initiation or response occurred, and a 0 if no initiation occurred and there was no opportunity for a response. If both an appropriate and inappropriate interaction occurred, record a + and −.

Interactions: Record a 1 if an interaction occurred and a 0 if an interaction did not occur.

Another recording procedure is momentary time sampling. In this method, the teacher sets an interval (e.g., 10 s) and records if the behavior occurred at the end of that interval. This method is less effective for lower frequency behaviors. Ms. Rosie has decided to use partial interval recording to observe Riley. Because Riley rarely initiates, Ms. Rosie is worried that she may miss some important information using momentary time sampling.

Step 2: Identifying motivating consequences. Individuals socially interact for a reason. For students with ASD or other DD, the reason or social goal may not be readily apparent because behaviors used to achieve these goals can be unexpected and obscure intent. As a result, some coding schemes attempt to identify what happens before and after an interaction to determine what motivates or reinforces the interaction (Boyd et al., 2011; Brown et al., 1996; Conroy & Brown, 2002; Conroy et al., 2007). For example, Ms. Coffey observed Joseph on the playground and found that he frequently initiated toward his peers, but that these initiations were about a preferred topic: maps. Joseph's peers responded, but often left the conversation quickly. When a peer left the conversation, Joseph immediately sought a new peer and again initiated a discussion about maps. In this observation, it became clear to Ms. Coffey that in addition to talking about maps, Joseph really enjoyed getting attention from his peers even though it was brief and occasionally negative. In contrast, Ms. Rosie found that Riley never initiated toward her peers, but she happily played alone next to them. Riley occasionally invented her own play that peers found interesting, and they initiated toward Riley to play. Although Riley never protested, she ignored her peers' initiations and when she did respond she imitated their play behavior.

Both Ms. Coffey and Ms. Rosie can use this information to help plan a social intervention. For example, Ms. Coffey may decide to target turn taking and perspective taking for Joseph to increase his initiations and maintain interactions with his peers. Because Riley seems interested in play and the actions of her peers, and Riley's peers are interested in her, Ms. Rosie may plan a peer-mediated intervention to help Riley's peers successfully engage her in an interaction while also supporting Riley's communication so that she can effectively and meaningfully respond to peers. Therefore, we also recommend identifying the consequences that maintain students' appropriate or inappropriate social skills. By identifying consequences that reinforce appropriate social skills, we are likely to design more effective interventions.

Putting All the Pieces Together

Through this multiphase assessment process, teachers and school staff can gather all the data and develop a multicomponent, assessment-based intervention that matches the student's individual needs and strengths. Components of the plan should include (a) targeted social skills selected for instruction based on the student's strengths and needs and the appropriateness of the context, (b) antecedent factors that are likely to increase social exchanges (e.g., contexts, activities, materials, peers), and (c) consequences that serve as reinforcers and will increase the student's social skills. Once an individualized instructional program has been developed, teachers will want to use ongoing progress monitoring to evaluate the effectiveness of the intervention.

Supports and Resources

It can be difficult for teachers to observe social communication while providing instruction and support in the classroom. Other school personnel can be a good support when working on setting new intervention goals and monitoring progress. For example, school psychologists or special educators are great resources for setting up a progress monitoring system. Paraprofessionals, other school personnel, and volunteers can be helpful in recording data. A local university may have college students looking for service learning opportunities. Learning to code is a great skill to develop while also supporting a teacher. In addition, a number of applications for iPads/iPods are helpful in setting up a data collection system. Many of them have programs that can be used to create an interval recording system, which makes it easy for paraprofessionals, volunteers, or other support staff to help with data collection. Ms. Coffey set up her system using Behavior Tracker Pro, and her paraprofessional assists with collecting data during different interactive activities. Table 1.2 provides a few examples of data collection apps for the iPad and iPod.

Table 1.2
Behavior-Tracking Applications for iPad/iPod

Application	Web site	Description	Cost
ABC Data Pro	http://www.cbtaonline.com/drupal/welcome	Tracks frequency and interval data. Data is exported via e-mail and is accessible in Excel.	$27.99
Autism Tracker Pro	http://www.trackandshareapps.com/autism	Tracks and graphs frequency data. Exports graphs via e-mail, Dropbox, iCloud, or Twitter.	$9.99
Behavior LENS	http://www.behaviorlensapp.com	Tracks and graphs behavior. Used to collect frequency, duration, and interval data. Exports graphs via e-mail.	$29.99
Behavior Tracker Pro	http://www.behaviortrackerpro.com	Tracks and graphs behavior. Used to collect frequency, duration, and interval data. Data is exported via e-mail and is accessible in Excel.	$29.99
iBehavewell	http://www.ibehavewell.com/ibehavewell.com/welcome.html	Tracks frequency data. Data is graphed and exported via e-mail.	$0.99
Intervals, duration, and frequency apps	http://www.elocinsoft.com/intervals	elocinSoft has three applications available. One collects interval data ($9.99), one duration data ($4.99), and the third frequency data ($0.99). Data is exported via e-mail, iTunes, or Dropbox, and is accessible in Excel.	$0.99 $4.99 $9.99

References

American Psychiatric Association. (2013). *Diagnostic and statistical manual of mental disorders* (5th ed.). Arlington, VA: Author.

Boyd, B. A., Conroy, M. A., Asmus, J., & McKenney, E. (2011). Direct observation of peer-related social interaction: Outcomes for young children with autism spectrum disorders. *Exceptionality, 19*, 94–108. http://dx.doi.org/10.1080/09362835.2011.565724

Boyd, B., Conroy, M. A., Mancil, G. R., Nakao, T., & Alter, P. J. (2007). Effects of circumscribed interests on the social behaviors of children with autism spectrum disorders: Use of structural analysis analogues. *Journal of Autism and Developmental Disorders, 37*, 1550–1561. http://dx.doi.org/10.1007/s10803-006-0286-8

Brown, W. H., & Conroy, M. A. (2002). Promoting peer-related social-communicative competence in preschool children. In H. Goldstein, L. Kaczmarek, & K. M. English (Eds.), *Promoting social communication in children and youth with developmental disabilities* (pp. 173–210). Baltimore, MD: Brookes.

Brown, W. H., & Conroy, M. A. (2012). Social-emotional competence in young children with developmental delays: Our reflection and vision for the future. *Journal of Early Intervention, 33*, 310–320. http://dx.doi.org/10.1177/1053815111429969

Brown, W. H., Odom, S. L., & Conroy, M. (2001). An intervention hierarchy for promoting preschool children's peer interactions in natural environments. *Topics in Early Childhood Special Education, 21*, 162–175. http://dx.doi.org/10.1177/027112140102100304

Brown, W. H., Odom, S. L., & Holcombe, A. (1996). Observational assessment of young children's social behavior with peers. *Early Childhood Research Quarterly, 11*, 19–40. http://dx.doi.org/10.1016/s0885-2006(96)90027-7

Brown, W. H., Odom, S. L., & McConnell, S. R. (2008). *Social competence of young children: Risk, disability, and evidence-based practices* (2nd ed.). Baltimore, MD: Brookes.

Buysse, V. (1993). Friendships of preschoolers with disabilities in community-based child care settings. *Journal of Early Intervention, 17*, 380–395. http://dx.doi.org/ 10.1177/105381519301700404

Chung, Y., & Carter, E. W. (2013). Promoting peer interactions in inclusive classrooms for students who use speech-generating devices. *Research & Practice for Persons with Severe Disabilities, 38*, 94–109. http://dx.doi.org/10.2511/027494813807714492

Conroy, M. A., Boyd, B. A., Asmus, J. M., & Madera, D. (2007). A functional approach for ameliorating social skills deficits in young children with autism spectrum disorders. *Infants and Young Children, 20*, 242–254. http://dx.doi.org/10.1097/01.iyc.0000277755.93313.7d

Conroy, M. A., & Brown, W. H. (2002). Preschool children: Putting research into practice. In H. Goldstein, L. Kaczmarek, & K. M. English (Eds.), *Promoting social communication in children and youth with developmental disabilities* (pp. 211–238). Baltimore, MD: Brookes.

Cunningham, A. B. (2012). Measuring change in social interaction skills of young children with autism. *Journal of Autism and Developmental Disorders, 42*, 593–605. http://dx.doi.org/10.1007/s10803-011-1280-3

Cutts, S., & Sigafoos, J. (2001). Social competence and peer interactions of students with intellectual disabilities in an inclusive high school. *Journal of Intellectual & Developmental Disabilities, 26,* 127–141. http://dx.doi.org/10.1080/13668250020054440

Delano, M., & Snell, M. E. (2006). The effects of social stories on the social engagement of children with autism. *Journal of Positive Behavior Interventions, 8,* 29–42. http://dx.doi.org/10.1177/10983007060080010501

English, K., Goldstein, H., Shafer, K., & Kaczmarek, L. (1997). Promoting interactions among preschoolers with and without disabilities. *Exceptional Children, 63,* 229–243.

Gena, A. (2006). The effects of prompting and social reinforcement on establishing social interactions with peers during the inclusion of four children with autism in preschool. *International Journal of Psychology, 41,* 541–554. http://dx.doi.org/10.1080/00207590500492658

Guralnick, M. J. (1990). Social competence and early intervention. *Journal of Early Intervention, 14,* 3–14. http://dx.doi.org/10.1177/105381519001400101

Guralnick, M. J. (2010). Early intervention approaches to enhance the peer-related social competence of young children with developmental delays: A historical perspective. *Infants & Young Children, 23*(2), 73–83. http://dx.doi.org/10.1097/iyc.0b013e3181d22e14

Guralnick, M. J., & Groom, J. M. (1987). The peer relations of mildly delayed and nonhandicapped preschool children in mainstreamed playgroups. *Child Development, 58,* 1556–1572. http://dx.doi.org/10.2307/1130695

Guralnick, M. J., Neville, B., Hammond, M. A., & Connor, R. T. (2007). The friendships of young children with developmental delays: A longitudinal analysis. *Journal of Applied Developmental Psychology, 28,* 64–79. http://dx.doi.org/10.1016/j.appdev.2006.10.004

Hartup, W. W., & Moore, S. G. (1990). Early peer relations: Developmental significance and prognostic implications. *Early Childhood Research Quarterly, 5,* 1–17. http://dx.doi.org/10.1016/0885-2006(90)90002-i

Kaczmarek, L. (2002). Assessment of social-communicative competence: An interdisciplinary model. In H. Goldstein, L. Kaczmarek, & K. M. English (Eds.), *Promoting social communication: Children with developmental disabilities from birth to adolescence* (pp. 55–115). Baltimore, MD: Brookes.

Kohler, F. W., Greteman, C., Raschke, D., & Highnam, C. (2007). Using a buddy skills package to increase the social interactions between a preschooler with autism and her peers. *Topics in Early Childhood Special Education, 27,* 155–163. http://dx.doi.org/10.1177/02711214070270030601

Lord, C., & McGee, J. P. (Eds.). (2001). *Educating children with autism. Committee on Educational Interventions for Children with Autism.* Washington, DC: National Academy Press.

Magnum, A., Fredrick, L., Pabico, R., & Roane, H. (2012). The role of context in the evaluation of reinforce efficacy: Implications for the preference assessment outcomes. *Research in Autism Spectrum Disorders, 6,* 158–167. http://dx.doi.org/10.1016/j.rasd.2011.04.001

McConnell, S. (2002). Intervention to facilitate social interaction for young children with autism: Review of available research and recommendations for educational intervention and future research. *Journal of Autism and Developmental Disorders, 32,* 351–372.

Murdock, L. C., Cost, H. C., & Tieso, C. (2007). Measurement of social communication skills of children with autism spectrum disorders during interactions with typical peers. *Focus on Autism and Other Developmental Disabilities, 22*(3), 160–172. http://dx.doi.org/10.1177/10883 576070220030301

Odom, S. L., McConnell, S. R., & Brown, W. H. (2008). Social competence of young children: Conceptualization, assessment, and influences. In W. H. Brown, S. L. Odom, & S. R. McConnell (Eds.), *Social competence for young children: Risk, disability, and intervention* (pp. 3–29). Baltimore, MD: Brookes.

Sigafoos, J., Schlosser, R. W., Green, V. A., O'Reilly, M., & Lancioni, G. E. (2008). Communication and social skill assessment. In J. Matson (Ed.), *Clinical assessment and intervention for autism spectrum disorders* (pp. 165–188). Boston, MA: Elsevier.

Stichter, J. P., & Conroy, M. A. (2006). *How to teach social skills and plan for peer social interactions.* Austin, TX: PRO-ED.

Theimann, K. S., & Goldstein, H. (2001). Social stories, written text cues, and video feedback: Effects on social communication of children with autism. *Journal of Applied Behavior Analysis, 34*, 425–446. http://dx.doi.org/10.1901/jaba.2001.34-425

Chapter **2**

Let's Play! Teaching Play Skills to Young Children
Mary Frances Hanline and Jennifer Riggie Ottley

Sachh is participating in a playgroup of twelve 4- and 5-year-old children in an outdoor area of an inclusive community early childhood education program. The program's monthly theme is water animals. Sachh and his peers are seated in a group on a wooden deck listening to the teacher, Jackie, read and talk about the book, Do Like a Duck Does! (Hindley, 2007). Sachh, seated at Jackie's feet, points to the book and says, "Quack, quack, quack." Jackie imitates the quacks and says, "See, the duck is biting the fox."

While Jackie reads, Bethena (an instructional aide) sets up play areas. One table on the deck has big plastic bins of water labeled with pictures of the items inside, a variety of plastic boats and water animals. Another is covered with books related to water animals, paper, and crayons. A sand play area contains shovels, buckets, and blocks; plastic alligators, turtles, and salamanders; and a hose to provide water to create mud. Another area is set up with two rows of four chairs and a single captain's chair to resemble a glass-bottom boat. A table near the boat contains two telephones, two computer keyboards, and a basket of tickets to be purchased for a boat ride. Bethena also makes dress-up clothes available, such as sun hats, sunglasses, boots, and flannel shirts.

After Jackie finishes the book, the children go to a play area of their choice. An airplane flies overhead, and Sachh covers his ears. When the plane is gone, Jackie says, "The airplane is gone, Sachh. You are fine. You can go play now." Sachh runs to Bethena, flapping his arms, and is helped to put on a flannel shirt. He runs off the deck, then returns when Bethena calls, "Come back, Sachh." When Sachh returns, Bethena reads a social script for the boating activity. Then she says, "Go buy a ticket and get on the boat" and points to where tickets can be purchased.

Sachh gets a ticket from the basket and says, "Ticket." Bethena encourages him to play, saying, "Give your ticket to Alexis and ride the boat." Sachh complies and seats himself on the boat along with two peers. Alexis brings a toy turtle to Sachh and asks if he wants the turtle. Sachh replies, "Ticket." Alexis says, "I'm going to be the driver," and returns to the captain's seat, yelling for everyone to hold onto their hats because the boat is leaving the dock. Sachh points to something on the playground and gets up, wandering around the deck area, talking to himself. After a few minutes, he points to the sand area and says, "Play lizard." He runs to the sand area and watches two other boys play in the sand. His peers continue to play in the sand.

Jordan, Sachh's play buddy, sees him alone by the sand and walks over with two plastic alligators. "Chomp chomp," says Jordan. "They are hungry. Sachh, let's find them something to eat." Jordan hands Sachh an alligator. Together they race over to a water bin filled with plastic fish. "Yummy fish," says Jordan as he dives his alligator into the bin. Sachh imitates Jordan's play, saying, "Eat, eat." Jordan and Sachh splash around the water and catch fish in their alligators' mouths, chomping and giggling. Jackie looks in their direction, smiles at their play, and exclaims, "I like the way Jordan and Sachh are playing together." Sachh looks up briefly, then continues playing with Jordan and the alligators: "Chomp, chomp."

The Importance of Play

The play activities in which Sachh and his peers engaged demonstrate the variety of ways play can promote development. Motor skills were practiced when Jordan and Sachh ran to play in the water bin filled with fish and when children picked a ticket from the basket to ride the glass-bottom boat. Social, communication, and problem-solving skills were learned as children negotiated their roles in the different play scenarios and interacted with one another and the teachers. Play is a means of expressing individual interests and developing a sense of self through emotional understanding, expression, and regulation, and play can act as a means of connecting with others and becoming a member of a community (Ashiabi, 2007).

Over the decades, prominent child developmental theorists have discussed the importance of play. For example, Piaget (1962) believed play provided a context in which children internalized new skills and prepared for their next learning spurt. Further, Vygotsky (1978) described play as the leading causal source of development in the preschool years because play serves as a scaffold by providing a natural social context in which children develop higher mental functions. Play is such a powerful influence in early development that it has been identified as the most developmentally appropriate context in which young children learn (Bredekamp & Copple, 1997) and has been referred to as the "integrative force" in early childhood curriculum (Hendrick, 2010). Studies have demonstrated that play enhances problem-solving abilities, cognitive functioning, representational competence, and divergent thinking (as reviewed in Burriss & Tsao, 2002); language development (e.g., Levy, Wolfgang, & Koorland, 1992); social participation (e.g., Lindsey & Colwell, 2003); literacy-related skills (e.g., Hanline, Milton, & Phelps, 2008); and mathematical readiness (e.g., Hanline et al, 2008).

Play and Its Development in Young Children

When Sachh and his peers interact with their physical and social environments, certain characteristics of their actions help define their behaviors as play. Play behaviors are accompanied by positive affect on the part of the children; play is pleasurable. Children are actively engaged in the activity and the engagement is process-oriented and intrinsically rewarding because children focus on the activity itself, not the goal, outcomes, or products of the activity. Play is imaginative and separated from the child's real world. Another characteristic of play is that it is freely chosen by the children (Johnson, Christie, & Wardle, 2005).

Play is further characterized by social and cognitive aspects of children's behavior (See Table 2.1). Stages of social play are often interpreted based on the work of Parten (1932), who viewed play as advancing from solitary to more social play. Advancement through the stages represents an increasing ability to interact with peers. Smilansky (1968) developed a frequently used categorization of children's cognitive play behaviors. Her work, based on Piagetian theory, divides play into functional play, constructive play, sociodramatic play, and games with rules. Each developmental stage reflects increasing representational thinking abilities.

Table 2.1
Social and Cognitive Aspects of Play

Aspects of play	Definition	Typical ages
Social aspects		
Unoccupied	No participation in play	All ages
Solitary	Plays alone; not using play material similar to those of peers	All ages
Onlooker	Watches peers play; may talk with peers, but does not enter into the play	1 to 3 years
Parallel	Plays alongside peers with similar play materials; no social interaction	2 ½ to 3 ½ years
Associative	Shares toys with peers; uses the same materials as peers; interacts with peers regarding play activity	3 ½ to 4 ½ years
Cooperative	Plays with peers with a shared purpose to the play activity; children have roles within the play	4 ½ to 6 years
Cognitive aspects		
Functional	Makes simple use of movements to provide exercise; learns about the physical characteristics of objects	Up to 3 years
Constructive	Works toward a goal of constructing things (e.g., stacks of blocks, an easel painting, a puzzle)	Up to 3 ½ years
Sociodramatic	Assumes roles; uses language and play for the purpose of pretending	4 to 6 ½ years
Games with rules	Understands and agrees to the structure and rules of a game	7 years and above

Note. Children may choose to play alone at certain times, although capable of more socially interactive behavior.

Play of Young Children With Developmental Disabilities and Autism Spectrum Disorder

Young children who have developmental disabilities (DD) and/or autism spectrum disorder (ASD) often exhibit delays in play development or a lack of specific skills needed to participate in play activities (Odom, McConnell, & Brown, 2008). Children with disabilities display less variety in their play and engage in fewer play behaviors than children developing typically (as reviewed in Lifter, Mason, & Barton, 2011). The play of young children with ASD has been described as simple and repetitive, lacking in the diversity and complexity of children without ASD (Honey, Leekam, Turner, & McConachie, 2007). In addition, children with ASD exhibit both delays in the development of symbolic play and lower levels of symbolic play (Rutherford & Rogers, 2003).

Teaching children to participate in play activities is a critical goal for young children with disabilities because knowing how to play increases the likelihood of placement in inclusive settings. Play is an intervention context into which systematic instruction can be embedded to teach a variety of skills; play also provides opportunities for children to practice, generalize, and maintain skills (Lifter, Mason, & Barton, 2011). However, systematic interventions are needed to teach play skills to young children with disabilities (Lifter, Ellis, Cannon, & Anderson, 2005).

Interventions to Enhance Play Skills

Play interventions can be used to teach skills necessary for participation in play activities. Skills necessary for such participation are the ability to (a) express interest, understanding, and emotions with peers; (b) join the play of others; and (c) participate in goal-oriented activities with peers (Lillvist, Sandberg, Bjorck-Akesson, & Granlund, 2009). In addition, children must be able to increase the complexity of their play skills over time (Jamison, Forston, & Stanton-Chapman, 2012). Thus, intervention should focus on both specific skill development (e.g., responding to a peer's initiation) and progression through the social and cognitive developmental stages. In Sachh's situation, he needed intervention to help him learn skills to be able to enter into the sand play of his peers, as well as support to help him develop more advanced sociodramatic skills as he and his peers played in the water. Many interventions incorporate the children's visual processing strengths, whereas others focus on social communication weaknesses.

Video Modeling

Video modeling is an intervention in which children or adults are video recorded modeling appropriate behaviors and verbalizations. For play interventions, the goal is for the child viewing the video to imitate the modeled behaviors when engaged in play (Reagon, Higbee, & Endicott, 2006). Videos may depict adults modeling appropriate play interactions from an observer's point of view or from the child's point of view (e.g., videos of the adult's hands manipulating the toys; Charlop, Dennis, Carpenter, & Greenberg, 2010). Video duration typically ranges from about 30 s to 4 min in length.

Video modeling has helped children use toys functionally, engage longer in sociodramatic play, and have more reciprocal play interactions (MacDonald, Sacramone, Mansfield, Wiltz, & Ahearn, 2009). It is helpful to model a variety of behaviors and verbalizations (i.e., generalization exemplars) that are considered appropriate for play (Charlop et al., 2010). These generalization exemplars help children use the play behaviors across settings. Video modeling can help improve the play skills of children with various abilities on the autism spectrum, but some research suggests that it takes an increased amount of intervention for children with more severe ratings on the Childhood Autism Rating Scale (Nikopoulos & Keenan, 2007).

Social Stories and Scripts

Social stories are short narratives that provide social cues and perspectives that describe a situation or skill (Gray, 2000). Social scripts are also narratives, but they provide the phrases, questions, and responses that script what the child should do or say. It is helpful to individualize stories and scripts for each child as well as for specific types of play behavior. Photographs and concrete play items are helpful tools for young children to better understand and acquire the target skill (Murdock & Hobbs, 2011). Teacher modeling and child role-play often accompany the use of social stories and scripts. Often, the intervention occurs with a teacher or peer just before the play session.

Although social stories and scripts have been used to support the play behaviors of children with various ability levels on the autism spectrum, they have only been used with children 4 years of age and older (e.g., Reagon & Higbee, 2009). These interventions have helped children with ASD or other DD increase the duration of time spent playing appropriately in preferred and nonpreferred play situations. In addition, children have improved in play behaviors such as social interactions, dialogues with peers, and choice making (Barry & Burlew, 2004; Conallen & Reed, 2012).

Visual Strategies

Conversation prompt cards, activity schedules, and visual task organization provide helpful support for children with ASD in play situations. Conversation prompt cards are typically used with children who have some reading abilities. The cards contain words or phrases accompanied by pictures that describe topics for dialogue in a particular play context (Conallen & Reed, 2012). Before the child uses the prompt cards in a play setting, it may be helpful to practice communication based on the cards until the child can independently initiate and respond to communication based on the prompts (Ganz & Flores, 2008). In addition to improving children's communication from specific scripts on the prompt cards, children's context-related play interactions also tend to improve from the intervention (Ganz & Flores, 2008).

Visual schedules can be helpful in improving peer engagement and independent game play between children with disabilities and their peers (Betz, Higbee, & Reagon, 2008). Play schedules mirror typical activity schedules, but they outline the activities or steps for the specific play session. The schedules can be pictures, words, or a combination of both, with the goal being to provide children with information about what materials to use and what to do with them.

Visual schedules can be used alone, or they can be used as a part of task organization. Task organization is a four-component process focused on providing children with visual facts about an activity: information, instruction, organization, and clarity (See Figure 2.1). The information and instructions provided in visual form (e.g., a visual list of materials accompanied by pictures of functional play options for each item) are the first two components (Mavropoulou, Papadopoulou, & Kakana, 2011). The purpose of these sections is to provide information about the materials available and ideas about how children can use the toys in a new way. These two components can help increase the duration of time spent in play and extend the types of activities performed with the materials. The third component is visual organization of the materials, which entails providing all of the supplies necessary for the play activity and nothing that is unnecessary. This step does not require the addition of a visual; rather, when teachers plan the activity in advance and remove excess materials, children may find it easier to make use of the materials in a functional manner. The final component is visual clarity. This step requires the prior preparation of pictures depicting the steps of and/or goal of the play activity (Mavropoulou et al., 2011). It is helpful to provide additional information in these pictures that extends the instructions included in the visual schedule.

Figure 2.1
Task Organization for Park Play With LEGO® Bricks

Component 1: Visual information

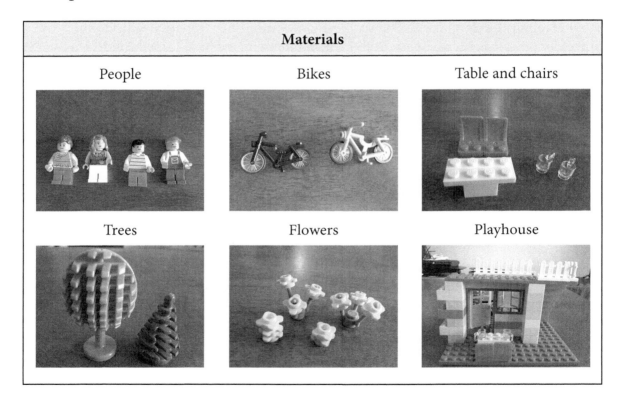

Figure 2.1 *(continued)*
Task Organization for Park Play With LEGO® Bricks

Component 2: Visual instruction

Playing at the park with my friend			
	Friend 1	**Friend 2**	
1.	Build the base of the play house (door, window, ladder, and walls).	Build the top of the play house and slide (red roof, safety rails, and slide).	
2.	Add the table and chairs.	Add the trees and flowers.	
	Both friends		
3.	Select a person and play on the top of the playhouse. Climb the ladder, use the slide, and cheer for your friend.		
4.	Ride bikes with your friend.		
5.	Take a break in the chairs or under the tree. Have a drink with the cups if you want to. Talk with your friend about the fun day.		

Figure 2.1 *(continued)*
Task Organization for Park Play With LEGO® Bricks

Component 2: Visual instruction

Playing at the park with my friend		
Both friends		
6.	Pretend play house with your friend.	
7.	Clean up your toys and put away.	

Component 3: Visual organization

Include the materials necessary for the activity and only those materials.	

Component 4: Visual clarity

Include the materials necessary for the activity and only those materials.	

Figure 2.1 *(continued)*
Task Organization for Park Play With LEGO® Bricks

Materials	Play options	
People only	Play tag	Talk to a friend
Trees	Walk around the trees	Rest in the shade
Flowers	Smell flowers	Pick flowers and give to a friend
Play house	Pretend play house	Climb the ladder

Figure 2.1 *(continued)*
Task Organization for Park Play With LEGO® Bricks

Materials	Play options	
Slide	Sliding down	Cheer for a friend sliding down
Table and seats	Have a drink	Sit down to rest
Bikes	Ride bikes	

Note. Models built of LEGO® bricks. LEGO® is a trademark of the LEGO Group of companies.

One schedule can be used for all children who have the same goal with the materials. For example, if children were playing with LEGO® bricks to build a park, the first component could contain pictures and words that describe a park and examples of play in the park. The second component could be a visual schedule of the items to construct. The third component would require the teacher to place the LEGO® bricks needed to construct the park in a container and remove any not required. The fourth component would entail the teacher placing pictures of the pieces to construct (e.g., bench, flower bed, and bike path), the completed park, and various activities occurring in the park (e.g., riding bike, buying food) in the container with the other materials. Although a new set of visuals would need to be created for a different play activity with the same types of materials (e.g., pirate ship or castle) or other toys (e.g., blocks or sand play), the process of task organization can help improve the on-task play behaviors for children with ASD or other DD during manipulative play and game play and, therefore, may be worth the extra preparation time required to develop the visual supports (Mavropoulou et al., 2011).

Physical and Social Environmental Arrangement

Providing choices in the context of play can motivate children to engage in play activities. Choices can include with whom to play, with what materials to play, or what to do with the materials provided. When selecting highly motivating play activities, the use of preference assessments can be helpful in determining preferred and nonpreferred items and activities (Cannella-Malone, Sabielny, Jimenez, & Miller, 2013; Conallen & Reed, 2012). Providing children with ASD or other DD materials and activities that are of high interest can increase the amount of time spent engaged in play individually and with peers (Farr, Yuill, & Raffle, 2010; Kohler, Greteman, Raschke, & Highnam, 2007). Other techniques, such as providing a reason for play and talking about the play activity as it is occurring, may also increase the duration of time spent playing, engaged in functional play, and socializing with others (Stagnitti, O'Connor, & Sheppard, 2012).

Getting close to children and following their lead in play may help foster more socialization as well as shared attention and interactions throughout the play activity (Kasari, Freeman, & Paparella, 2006). For example, consider a 5-year-old child with ASD standing next to peers engaged in easel-painting. The child with ASD is making up-and-down paint marks by scrubbing the brush onto the paper with one color of paint. Her peers are drawing simple butterflies and trees using multiple colors. When following the child's lead, the adult approaches the child and labels the behavior of the child ("I see you are painting at the easel."). The teacher begins to paint with the child and imitate brush strokes in a reciprocal fashion while continuing to label actions. Then, the teacher begins to scaffold the play by modeling and labeling more developmentally sophisticated behaviors. In this example, the teacher could model making a cross or a circle and use different colors while encouraging the child to imitate her ("Can you paint a cross on the paper?" "Let's use the blue paint now.").

Embedded Systematic Intervention Strategies Within Play

Embedding behavioral strategies into play routines can have positive impacts on the rate that children with ASD or other DD play and communicate with their peers. These strategies can improve children's social-play behaviors (e.g., sharing) and emotional skills (e.g., giving compliments), and help build better friendships (DeQuinzio, Townsend, & Poulson, 2008). Behavioral techniques have supported the learning of children with disabilities for about 50 years, and these evidence-based techniques can be embedded into play activities to support children to develop, maintain, and generalize play skills (Stahmer, Ingersoll, & Carter, 2003).

Verbal, gestural, and physical prompting provide a reminder for children to play in appropriate ways and/or meet their targeted play goals. Time delay can occur in constant or increasing increments and provide more consistent prompts and feedback to children about their goals. The amount of time that adults wait to provide prompts varies, but it is helpful to pre-establish the increment and have a signal or cue to remind the adult to give a prompt if the child is not performing the target play behavior (Licciardello, Harchik, & Luiselli (2008).

Prompting and time delay are helpful tools if the child is learning a discrete behavior. If the behavior requires multiple steps to complete (e.g., approaching a peer and asking to play), then chaining procedures can provide the supports needed (Liber, Frea, & Symon, 2008). Chaining allows the complex skill to be mastered one step at a time. Instruction and support can be provided on each step as needed until the child can perform the entire behavior independently.

Reinforcement and modeling can be provided by either adults or other children and are helpful for both discrete and complex play behaviors. Often reinforcement is provided contingently for correctly performed behaviors, and some adults have found it helpful to give corrective feedback when reinforcement is not warranted (Leaf et al., 2009). When modeling behaviors, adults may purposely leave out an important component of the behavior and ask the child to provide input about the adult model, helping the adult gauge whether the child understands the complete correct behavior (Oppenheim-Leaf, Leaf, Dozier, Sheldon, & Sherman, 2012). It is important to provide a complete and correct model of the target behavior before the child is expected to practice it.

Group Interventions

Group interventions provide the opportunity for children to learn from one another. Group interventions tend to improve the duration of cooperative play and frequency of appropriate social interactions directly in the play context as well as other generalized contexts not targeted for intervention (Frankel, Gorospe, Chang, & Sugar, 2011). For adults (parents or professionals) facilitating a play date or play group, it is important to provide training on the strategies helpful in improving targeted child behaviors. Reviewing the strategies before the play session and/or receiving feedback from a coach on the strategies may help adults use the strategies more regularly (Zercher, Hunt, Schuler, & Webster, 2001). Training is also helpful for interventions with other children as the facilitators. Practices such as child role-play help ensure that the children have mastered the skills desired for play contexts when they are playing with the child who has a disability (Oppenheim-Leaf et al., 2012).

Combined Interventions

Many children can successfully improve their play skills by combining components of the interventions. Frequently, visual interventions or behavioral strategies are used as supports for children in group interventions. These supports help peers implement the strategies accurately and encourage the strategies' continued usage after a timeframe for implementation has elapsed (Zercher et al., 2001). They can also help children with ASD or other DD engage in more functional play and exhibit more social behaviors with their peers (Thomas & Smith, 2004).

Many combination intervention packages focus on the children's play skills and the children's social-communication development (e.g., Dykstra, Boyd, Watson, Crais, & Baranek, 2012). These interventions tend to include adult modeling of both play and language skills as well as oral descriptions about the play context (e.g., Gillett & LeBlanc, 2007). Combined interventions have the ability to increase the appropriateness of children's play as well as the children's play diversity and sophistication; additional benefits of combined interventions include improvements in joint attention, joint engagement, language, and social skills (Kasari et al., 2006; Stagnitti et al., 2012). These outcomes suggest that combined interventions may help to improve other developmental areas that are typically delayed in children with ASD or other DD.

Intervention Application

The interventions described could be used in Sachh's preschool to increase social interactions within the play activities and the developmental level of Sachh's play. Table 2.2 provides suggestions for using each intervention to support Sachh. As Sachh increases his social skills, the interventions can support his moving to more sophisticated social and cognitive developmental levels (Jamison, 2010). The video modeling intervention, for example, could be changed from modeling function play to modeling constructive play in the sand.

Table 2.2
Intervention Application for Sachh

Intervention	Example for Sachh	Additional resources
Video modeling	Before going outside, have Sachh view a video of appropriate sand play with a shovel, bucket, and a few amphibians. While Sachh is observing his peers play with the lizard in the sand, Jackie could remind him about the video they watched together and encourage him to join in play with his peers.	Overview of video modeling, implementation steps, and checklist http://autismpdc.fpg.unc.edu/content/video-modeling 10 tips for making videos http://www.socialskillbuilder.com/tips-for-making-videos.htm
Social stories and scripts	After Bethena reads the social script to Sachh on the deck, Sachh could practice the script one or two times with Bethena before she encourages him to buy a ticket. This practice could help promote appropriate socialization with his peers during the interaction.	Autism Internet Module for all types of social narratives http://www.autisminternetmodules.org/mod_intro.php?mod_id=18 Tip sheet for making social narratives http://csefel.vanderbilt.edu/scriptedstories/tips.pdf Steps for implementation http://www.autisminternetmodules.org/up_doc/SocialNarrativesSteps10-31-08.pdf

Table 2.2 *(continued)*
Intervention Application for Sachh

Intervention	Example for Sachh	Additional resources
Other visual strategies	After Sachh got a ticket to ride the boat, Bethena could give Sachh a conversation prompt card. Bethena could point to the three pictures one at a time and have Sachh tell her what he should talk about for that cue. If Sachh struggles to remember the scripts, Bethena could remind him of the scripts and encourage him to use them during play on the boat.	Conversation prompt card template http://www.handsinautism.org/pdf/How_To_Topic_Boards.pdf Activity schedule tip sheet http://www.haringcenter.washington.edu/sites/default/files/file/ActivityScheduleTipSheet.pdf Visual supports (AIM module) http://www.autisminternetmodules.org/mod_intro.php?mod_id=2
Environmental arrangement	Before Sachh left the reading circle to go play, Jackie could give him three specific options of with whom or what to play. This may help reduce latency in initiating a play activity.	Environmental arrangement strategies http://www.dec-sped.org/uploads/docs/conference/2012%20Handouts/PRA299_Environmental_Arrangement.pdf
Embedded behavioral strategies	Jackie can set a timer on her watch to beep at 1-min intervals. This could be her cue to check on Sachh and provide him with reinforcement, corrective feedback, or prompts. This technique can help Jackie provide Sachh with feedback more consistently.	CONNECT module 1: Embedded interventions http://community.fpg.unc.edu/connect-modules/learners/module-1 Overview of prompting http://autismpdc.fpg.unc.edu/content/prompting

Table 2.2 *(continued)*
Intervention Application for Sachh

Intervention	Example for Sachh	Additional resources
Group interventions	Jordan did a wonderful job initiating play with his play buddy Sachh. As more play and social skills become targets for Sachh, teach these to Jordan along with strategies that Jordan can use to foster Sacch's skills.	Steps for implementation of social skills groups http://autismpdc.fpg.unc.edu/sites/autismpdc.fpg.unc.edu/files/SocSkillsGroups_Steps.pdf Setting up a successful play date http://www.autismtherapies.com/uploads/Play_date_tip_sheet.pdf
Preference assessments	Sachh loves playing outdoors and resists making the transition to his next activity indoors. The teachers previously conducted a preference assessment by providing Sachh with materials from each of the activities available to Sachh indoors: microdramatic play, sociodramatic play, and readiness. They observed that he interacted longest with materials from the microdramatic center (i.e., miniature people, animals, buildings, vehicles). When it is time to go inside, the teacher shows Sachh a picture of the microdramatic play area and tells him he may play with the materials pictured indoors after he has helped clean up outside.	Preference and reinforcer assessment http://touchautism.com/Preference%20and%20Reinforcer%20Assessment.aspx Conducting an informal preference assessment (includes video of 6-year old with ASD) http://www.baam.emich.edu/baammoviepages/BAAMmgchoosing.htm

Final Thoughts

Young children with ASD or other DD can benefit from participation in play activities with peers. Play provides opportunities to increase skills across all developmental domains in an integrated fashion. Playing with peers can also provide opportunities to develop a sense of belonging, which is a critical goal for young children with disabilities (Cook, Klein, & Chen, 2012). However, in order for children with disabilities to benefit from the interactions that occur during play and to continue to progress developmentally in play skills, systematic intervention is needed. A variety of evidence-based practices provide guidance to teachers. Many of the practices described in this chapter utilize the strengths exemplified by most children with ASD or other DD (i.e., processing visual information and functioning in structured environments). The practices enable teachers to create an environment in which play skills can be developed and used in natural environments, thus promoting increased diversity, sophistication, and engagement in play as well as improving the likelihood for improved relations with peers (e.g., Stagnitti et al., 2012).

References

Ashiabi, G. (2007). Play in the preschool classroom: Its socioemotional significance and the teacher's role in play. *Early Childhood Education Journal, 35*, 199–207. http://dx.doi.org/10.1007/s10643-007-0165-8

Barry, L. M., & Burlew, S. B. (2004). Using social stories to teach choice and play skills to children with autism. *Focus on Autism and Other Developmental Disabilities, 19*, 45–51. http://dx.doi.org/10.1177/10883576040190010601

Betz, A., Higbee, T. S., & Reagon, K. A. (2008). Using joint activity schedules to promote peer engagement in preschoolers with autism. *Journal of Applied Behavior Analysis, 41*, 237–241. http://dx.doi.org/10.1901/jaba.2008.41-237

Bredekamp, S., & Copple, C. (1997). *Developmentally appropriate practice in early childhood programs* (Rev. ed.). Washington, DC: National Association for the Education of Young Children.

Burriss, K. G., & Tsao, L. L. (2002). Review of research: How much do we know about the importance of play in child development? *Childhood Education, 78*, 230–233. http://dx.doi.org/10.1080/00094056.2002.10522188

Cannella-Malone, H., Sabielny, L., Jimenez, E. D., Miller, M. M. (2013). Pick one! Conducting preference assessments with students with significant disabilities. *TEACHING Exceptional Children, 45*, 6-15. http://dx.doi.org/ 10.1177/004005991304500601

Charlop, M. H., Dennis, B., Carpenter, M. H., & Greenberg, A. L. (2010). Teaching socially expressive behaviors to children with autism through video modeling. *Education and Treatment of Children, 33*, 371–393. http://dx.doi.org/10.1353/etc.0.0104

Conallen, K., & Reed, P. (2012). The effects of a conversation prompt procedure on independent play. *Research in Autism Spectrum Disorders, 6*, 365–377. http://dx.doi.org/10.1016/j.rasd.2011.06.010

Cook, R. E., Klein, M. D., & Chen, D. (2012). *Adapting early childhood curricula for children with special needs* (8th ed.). Upper Saddle River, NJ: Pearson.

DeQuinzio, J. A., Townsend, D. B., & Poulson, C. L. (2008). The effects of forward chaining and contingent social interaction on the acquisition of complex sharing responses by children with autism. *Research in Autism Spectrum Disorders, 2,* 264–275. http://dx.doi.org/10.1016/j.rasd.2007.06.006

Dykstra, J. M., Boyd, B. A., Watson, L. R., Crais, E. R., & Baranek, G. T. (2012). The impact of the advancing social-communication and play (ASAP) intervention on preschoolers with autism spectrum disorders. *Autism, 16,* 27–44. http://dx.doi.org/10.1177/1362361311408933

Farr, W., Yuill, N., & Raffle, H. (2010). Social benefits of a tangible user interface for children with autistic spectrum conditions. *Autism, 14,* 237–252. http://dx.doi.org/10.1177/1362361310363280

Frankel, F. D., Gorospe, C. M., Chang, Y., & Sugar, C. A. (2011). Mothers' reports of play dates and observation of school playground behavior of children having high-functioning autism spectrum disorders. *Journal of Child Psychology and Psychiatry, 52,* 571–579. http://dx.doi.org/10.1111/j.1469-7610.2010.02318

Ganz, J. B., & Flores, M. M. (2008). Effects of the use of visual strategies in play groups for children with autism spectrum disorders and their peers. *Journal of Autism and Developmental Disorders, 38,* 926–940. http://dx.doi.org/10.1007/s10803-007-0463-4

Gillett, J. N., & LeBlanc, L. A. (2007). Parent-implemented natural language paradigm to increase language and play in children with autism. *Research in Autism Spectrum Disorders, 1,* 247–255. http://dx.doi.org/10.1016/j.rasd.2006.09.003

Gray, C. (2000). *The new social story book.* Arlington, TX: Future Horizons.

Hanline, M. F., Milton, S., & Phelps, P. C. (2008). A longitudinal study exploring the relationship of representational levels of three aspects of preschool sociodramatic play and early academic skills. *Journal of Research in Childhood Education, 23*(1), 19–28. http://dx.doi.org/10.1080/02568540809594643

Hendrick, J. (2010). *Total learning: Developmental curriculum for the young child* (7th ed.). Upper Saddle River, NJ: Pearson.

Hindley, J. (2007). *Do like a duck does!* Somerville, MA: Candlewick.

Honey, E., Leekam, S., Turner, M., & McConachie, H. (2007). Repetitive behavior and play in typically developing children and children with autism spectrum disorders. *Journal of Autism and Developmental Disorders, 37,* 1107–1115. http://dx.doi.org/10.1007/s10803-006-0253-4

Jamison, K. R. (2010). Effects of a social communication intervention for promoting social competence through play in young children with disabilities. *Dissertation Abstracts International: Section A, 72*(4), Publication No. AAT 3445589.

Jamison, K. R., Forston, L. D., & Stanton-Chapman, T. L. (2012). Encouraging social skill development through play in early childhood special education classrooms. *Young Exceptional Children, 15*(2), 3–19. http://dx.doi.org/10.1177/1096250611435422

Johnson, J. E., Christie, J. F., & Wardle, F. (2005). *Play, development, and early education.* Boston, MA: Allyn & Bacon.

Kasari, C., Freeman, C., & Paparella, T. (2006). Joint attention and symbolic play in young children with autism: A randomized controlled intervention study. *Journal of Child Psychology and Psychiatry, 47,* 611–620. http://dx.doi.org/10.1111/j.1469-7610.2005.01567.x

Kohler, F. W., Greteman, C., Raschke, D., & Highnam, C. (2007). Using a buddy skills package to increase the social interactions between a preschooler with autism and her peers. *Topics in Early Childhood Special Education, 27,* 155–163. http://dx.doi.org/10.1177/02711214070270030601

Leaf, J. B., Taubman, M., Bloomfield, S., Palos-Rafuse, L., Leaf, R., McEachin, J., & Oppenhein, M. L. (2009). Increasing social skills and pro-social behavior for three children diagnosed with autism through the use of a teaching package. *Research in Autism Spectrum Disorders, 3,* 275-289. http://dx.doi.org/10.1016/j.rasd.2008.07.003

Levy, A. K., Wolfgang, C., & Koorland, M. (1992). Sociodramatic play as a method for enhancing the language performance of kindergarten age students. *Early Childhood Research Quarterly 7,* 245–262. http://dx.doi.org/10.1016/0885-2006(92)90007-l

Liber, D. B., Frea, W. D., & Symon, J. B. (2008). Using time-delay to improve social play skills with peers for children with autism. *Journal of Autism and Developmental Disorders, 38,* 312–323. http://dx.doi.org/10.1007/s10803-007-0395-z

Licciardello, C. C., Harchik, A. E., & Luiselli, J. K. (2008). Social skills intervention for children with autism during interactive play at a public elementary school. *Education and Treatment of Children, 31,* 27–37. http://dx.doi.org/10.1353/etc.0.0010

Lifter, K., Ellis, J., Cannon, B., & Anderson, S. R. (2005). Developmental specificity in targeting and teaching play activities to children with pervasive developmental disorders. *Journal of Early Intervention, 27,* 247–267. http://dx.doi.org/10.1177/105381510502700405

Lifter, K., Mason, E. J., & Barton, E. E. (2011). Children's play: Where we have been and where we could go. *Journal of Early Intervention, 33,* 281–297. http://dx.doi.org/10.1177/1053815111429465

Lillvist, A., Sandberg, A., Bjorck-Akesson E., & Granlund, M. (2009). Special support in preschools in Sweden: Preschool staff's definition of the construct. *International Journal of Disability, Development, and Education, 57,* 43-47.

Lindsey, E. W., & Colwell, M. J. (2003). Preschoolers' emotional competence: Links to pretend and physical play. *Child Study Journal, 33*(1), 39–52.

MacDonald, R., Sacramone, S., Mansfield, R., Wiltz, K., & Ahearn, W. H. (2009). Using video modeling to teach reciprocal pretend play to children with autism. *Journal of Applied Behavior Analysis, 42,* 43–55. http://dx.doi.org/10.1901/jaba.2009.42-43

Mavropoulou, S., Papadopoulou, E., & Kakana, D. (2011). Effects of task organization on the independent play of students with autism spectrum disorders. *Journal of Autism and Developmental Disorders, 41,* 913–925. http://dx.doi.org/10.1007/s10803-010-1116-6

Murdock, L. C., & Hobbs, J. Q. (2011). Picture me playing: Increasing pretend play dialogue of children with autism spectrum disorders. *Journal of Autism and Developmental Disorders, 41,* 870–878. http://dx.doi.org/10.1007/s10803-010-1108-6

Nikopoulos, C. K., & Keenan, M. (2007). Using video modeling to teach complex social sequences to children with autism. *Journal of Autism and Developmental Disorders, 37,* 678–693. http://dx.doi.org/10.1007/s10803-006-0195-x

Odom, S. L., McConnell, S. R., & Brown, W. H. (2008). Social competence of young children: Conceptualization, assessment, and influences. In W. H. Brown, S. L. Odom, & S. R. McConnell (Eds.), *Social competence of young children: Risk, disability, and intervention* (pp. 3–29). Baltimore, MD: Brookes.

Oppenheim-Leaf, M. L., Leaf, J. B., Dozier, C., Sheldon, J. B., & Sherman, J. A. (2012). Teaching typically developing children to promote social play with their siblings with autism. *Research in Autism Spectrum Disorders, 6,* 77–791. http://dx.doi.org/10.1016/j.rasd.2011.10.010

Parten, M. B. (1932). Social participation among preschool children. *Journal of Abnormal and Social Psychology 27,* 243–269. http://dx.doi.org/10.1037/h0074524

Piaget, J. (1962). *Play, dreams, and imitation in childhood.* New York, NY: Norton Press.

Reagon, K. A., & Higbee, T. S. (2009). Parent-implemented script fading to promote play-based verbal initiations in children with autism. *Journal of Applied Behavior Analysis, 42,* 659–664. http://dx.doi.org/10.1901/jaba.2009.42-659

Reagon, K. A., Higbee, T. S., & Endicott, K. (2006). Teaching pretend play skills to a student with autism using video modeling with a sibling as model and play partner. *Education and Treatment of Children (West Virginia University Press), 29*(3), 517-528.

Rutherford, M. D., & Rogers, S. J. (2003). Cognitive underpinnings of pretend play in autism. *Journal of Autism and Developmental Disorders, 33,* 289–302.

Smilansky, S. (1968). *The effects of sociodramatic play on disadvantaged preschool children.* New York, NY: Wiley.

Stagnitti, K., O'Connor, C., & Sheppard, L. (2012). Impact of the learn to play program on play, social competence and language for children aged 5-8 years who attend a specialist school. *Australian Occupational Therapy Journal, 59,* 302–311. http://dx.doi.org/10.1111/j.1440-1630.2012.01018.x

Stahmer, A. C., Ingersoll, B., & Carter, C. (2003). Behavioral approaches to promoting play. *Autism, 7,* 401–413. http://dx.doi.org/10.1177/1362361303007004006

Thomas, N., & Smith, C. (2004). Developing play skills in children with autistic spectrum disorders. *Educational Psychology in Practice, 20*(3), 195-206.

Vygotsky, L. S. (1978). *Mind and society: The development of higher psychological processes.* Cambridge, MA: Harvard University Press.

Zercher, C., Hunt, P., Schuler, A., & Webster, J. (2001). Increasing joint attention, play, and language through peer supported play. *Autism, 5,* 374-398.

Chapter 3

Peer-Mediated Learning Strategies
Joshua Plavnick and Mari MacFarland

Peer-mediated learning strategies (PMLS) are evidence-based practices for teaching social interaction to individuals with developmental disabilities (DD; Reichow & Volkmar, 2010). PMLS involve teaching typically developing peers to interact with individuals with DD; peers and individuals with DD are then given opportunities to engage in social interactions (McConnell, 2002). The benefits of PMLS for children with DD include improved social competence, increased opportunities to interact with typical peers across multiple environments, positive models of social interaction, and independence (Sperry, Neitzel, & Engelhardt-Wells, 2010). These features often lead to the generalization of social interaction among individuals with DD, which is not an easily obtained outcome for this population (Bellini, Peters, Benner, & Hopf, 2007; Odom, Chandler, Ostrosky, McConnell, & Reaney, 1992). Peer-mediated learning strategies can also lead to academic gains, increased sensitivity to others, higher self-confidence, and expanded social networks among the typical peers involved in the intervention (Carter, Cushing, & Kennedy, 2008).

In addition to the benefits for children, PMLS provide a practical benefit for educators of individuals with DD (Carter et al., 2008). As the number of students with DD continues to increase, it is not practical to expect that one adult can provide all the instruction necessary for this group of learners. In addition, demands on teachers to deliver academic instruction decrease the amount of time educators have available to explicitly focus on social interaction skills, although learners with DD often require explicit and frequent instruction in social interaction. By training peers in the child's environment to be social skills teachers, an educator can embed explicit instruction in social interaction throughout a child's day without compromising requirements to provide requisite academic instruction. Thus, the optimal outcome of PMLS is that all parties benefit from being involved in the process (Carter et al., 2008).

Overview of the Evidence for Peer-Mediated Learning Strategies

PMLS are supported by an extensive research base for children with DD and can be used across a range of ages or settings and to teach a variety of target behaviors (Sperry et al., 2010; see also Goldstein, Kaczmarek, Pennington, & Shafer, 1992; Odom & Strain, 1986; Sainato, Goldstein, & Strain, 1992). Research has shown the efficacy of the intervention for children from preschool through high school; in private, public, clinical, and community-based settings; and with individuals across the spectrum of disability severity (Sperry et al., 2010). Procedural modifications can be made for a young child with a severe disability, who likely receives one-to-one peer mediation, versus an adolescent with a mild disability, who might participate in a social skills group with several typical peers and other peers with similar disabilities. Ultimately, PMLS can be used in combination with many other focused or comprehensive interventions for individuals with DD and should be incorporated into the educational programs of all children and adolescents with DD (Reichow & Volkmar, 2010).

PMLS can be implemented using a variety of procedural configurations and arrangements that offer increased opportunities for the target students to practice and develop their social skills in a "real-life" setting where distractions and interruptions may take place. Peer-mediated learning strategies can be implemented in dyads (one typical peer and one student with DD) or small groups for all ages of students in a variety of settings. At the preschool level, PMLS often involves a dyadic process within the context of structured play activities (e.g., Thiemann & Kamps, 2008). However, at the high school level or for a child with a mild DD, PMLS are more likely to involve social networking strategies or group-based interventions involving multiple students with and without disabilities (e.g., Kamps et al., 1992).

PMLS are effective for teaching numerous social behaviors and can be customized based on the focal child's existing skills (Sperry et al., 2010). For example, whereas vocal initiations (e.g., starting a conversation) may be targeted for a child with intact expressive language (Pierce & Shreibman, 1995), gestural responding (e.g., waiving in response to a greeting) may be a target skill for a child who is not able to speak. The malleability of PMLS for a wide range of individuals with DD enhances its use as a focused intervention strategy. Through direct observation, educators can assess a child's existing social repertoire and select target behaviors appropriate for each student. Table 3.1 provides examples of some of the skills that have been targeted in previous research using PMLS. Skills are broken down based on age of the focal child.

Table 3.1
Examples of Target Skills for Students of Various Ages

Skills for younger students	Skills for secondary students
• Sharing items with others • Playing a basic game with a peer • Gaining a peer's attention • Showing an item to a peer or showing a peer how to complete an activity • Making and maintaining eye contact • Offering and accepting help	• Initiating a conversation with a peer • Asking and answering conversational questions • Maintaining conversations • Giving compliments and encouragement

Implementing PMLS

The successful implementation of PMLS requires several steps, each of which is outlined in Table 3.2 and explained in detail in the subsequent text. Unlike many intervention strategies (e.g., video modeling), prerequisites are not a concern prior to using PMLS because the procedures can be modified to meet a student's need. And because peers implement the interaction sessions, the majority of time for the teacher is spent in the preparation, data collection, and trouble-shooting stages.

Table 3.2
Implementing Peer-Mediated Learning Strategies

Step	Activity
1	Select peers
2	Select target skills
3	Select settings and materials
4	Prepare peers to interact with focal students
5	Prepare focal students for peer-mediated process
6	Administer interaction sessions
7	Collect data
8	Troubleshoot
9	Provide ongoing support to peers

Selecting Peers

The selection of typically developing peers for participation in PMLS is a critical component of the process and requires careful consideration and planning. Ideally, peer mediators should display appropriate social interaction skills, be well-liked by other peers, demonstrate consistent school attendance, have a positive (or at least neutral) social interaction history with the target student, demonstrate consistent completion of assigned work (to prevent them from falling behind if they miss an assignment due to participation in peer program), and demonstrate compliance with teacher instructions (e.g., Odom & Strain, 1986).

When selecting peers, it is also important to consider their interests and educational needs. It is optimal to partner a peer with a child with DD who shares a similar interest or preferred activity. In addition, multiple peers should be selected for each focal student to increase the likelihood of skill generalization and avoid burnout by a single peer mediator (Rogers, 2000).

At the preschool and elementary levels, educators identify one or two peers from within the same classroom as the target students (Carter et al., 2008). Teachers can extend invitations to specific students, make a request for peer volunteers, or utilize general announcements (e.g., flyers, school-home communication sheets). When explaining to peers what a peer mediated project entails, the teacher will want to explain the types of activities, the amount of time activities will last, and how often the structured interactions will occur. Rather than focusing on the target student's disability with preschool and elementary school children, it may be more effective to focus on describing the program as a chance for everyone to "make new friends" (Thiemann & Kamps, 2008). It is important to discuss the program with parents of typical children who may be involved. After discussing the program with parents and based on individual school policies, it may be beneficial to create a "buddy contract" that peers can read and sign, indicating that they want to be buddies. An example of a buddy contract is depicted in Figure 3.1.

Figure 3.1
Example of a Peer-Buddy Contract for Young Children

Many of the guidelines for the selection of peers at the preschool and elementary levels also apply to the secondary level. For example, a successful peer mediator in a secondary setting should be well-liked by his or her peers, display good social skills, and be willing to participate in the PMLS (Carter & Kennedy, 2006). In addition, multiple peers should be recruited to provide ongoing social support to classmates with social skills deficits (Carter et al., 2008). A unique consideration for peers at the secondary level is to include peers who transition from one setting to another (e.g., course to course) with the focal students. Transition times between classes or activities can be stressful for students with DD and often involve many opportunities for social interaction that students with DD may be left out of if not otherwise supported. Recruiting one or more peers to accompany a student with DD at passing times is an ideal way to incorporate PMLS throughout the day at the secondary level.

One of the biggest obstacles to peer selection at the secondary level is recruitment because students do not remain in the classroom or with the same teacher for the entire day. It may be helpful from a recruitment perspective to select a distinctive name for the program (e.g., "Peer Connections") to avoid confusion with existing programs already running in a particular school or district. Many districts have peer mediation programs that involve teams of typically developing peers who work toward win-win resolutions in situations where students have gotten into trouble for a variety of reasons (e.g., fighting, social media improprieties, rumor and gossip, bullying; Thompson, 1996). Due to potential similarities in program names, it may be important to distinguish a PMLS program from existing programs within a building or district.

Colleagues (e.g., the student activities director, honor society advisor, general education teachers, sports team coaches, music, drama, and art teachers) who regularly interact with a diverse group of typical peers can disseminate information and be excellent partners in the recruitment process. In addition, school administrators can help facilitate the recruitment process and in some cases may support the delivery of elective credits for peers who choose to get involved. It can also be helpful to arrange school announcements, distribute flyers, post articles in the school newspaper, or create t-shirts for students who become involved in the program. Eventually, word of mouth can be the best recruitment tool; as students agree to participate and discuss the program with others, several more students might elect to get involved in the program.

After peers have been recruited at the secondary level, it is recommended that teachers utilize screening procedures, including a written application in which the student identifies educators who can provide a reference on behalf of the peer (e.g., a guidance counselor or teacher; Hughes & Carter, 2008). The application might also ask students to share their reasons for wanting to be a peer mediator and previous experiences interacting with individuals with disabilities.

Selecting Target Skills

The selection of target skills is important from the perspective of the peer mediator and the focal student. Because the emphasis in PMLS involves social interaction, each target skill essentially involves at least two components: one that is performed by the peer mediator and the other by the focal student. Consideration of the skills that the focal student will acquire as a result of the intervention guides other aspects of the procedures, including selection of the setting, training the peer, and planning to collect data. In addition, the presence of problematic behavior for the focal student must be considered. For example, if a student with DD is argumentative or aggressive when interacting with peers, the practitioner could focus on using an appropriate tone of voice, perspective-taking, or recognizing and controlling one's own emotions.

The child's levels of social competence should be considered prior to selecting target behaviors. Assessment of social competence can involve direct observation of specific behaviors or indirect checklists of global social behavior (e.g., Social Skills Improvement System – Rating Scales; Gresham & Elliott, 2008). Children who lack basic social behaviors such as orienting toward others when interacting, taking turns, and responding to initiations of others should learn these skills prior to targeting more complex behavior, such as initiating or maintaining conversation.

Another factor that can influence skill acquisition is the interrelation between the complexity of the target behavior and the consequences that occur as a result of that behavior. For example, it is often easier for children with DD to respond to peers' initiations rather than initiate an interaction with a peer. However, if the focal student is taught to initiate with his peer by asking for a turn with a highly preferred toy, he may learn the skill very quickly after experiencing the consequences for an accurate response. If so, it may be optimal to begin the peer-mediated intervention by teaching the focal child to initiate with, as opposed to respond to, his peer. Initiating by commenting about a toy, on the other hand, may not produce a similar naturally occurring preferred consequence and could therefore require alternative methods of motivation (i.e., contrived reinforcement). Generally speaking, practitioners must consider the amount of effort required to perform social interactions, consequences for engaging in the target behavior, and the interaction between these two factors.

Case Vignette: Selecting Target Behaviors

Ms. Garfield is a special education teacher who co-teaches with a general education language arts teacher in a ninth-grade English class of 20 students ranging from 13 to 15 years old. Nine students within Ms. Garfield and her co-teacher's class have various disabilities and receive special education services. One of the nine students, Sandra, is diagnosed with autism spectrum disorder and has notable deficits in social skills. Although Sandra attends general education classes throughout her entire school day, she has minimal social interactions with her peers.

Through informal observations of Sandra, Ms. Garfield has noticed that Sandra spends almost all of her passing and lunch time with one other student, Jen, who is diagnosed with intellectual disability and also displays social skills deficits. Sandra and Jen appear to have reciprocal conversations, but Jen does most of the talking, and Sandra often engages in other activities, such as drawing, while Jen is talking. Ms. Garfield has observed Sandra laugh during interactions with Jen, but the laughter does not appear to be related to the conversation.

Ms. Garfield has also observed that Sandra engages in few initiations with typically developing peers who are seated in close proximity to her. When she does initiate, Sandra will typically make one statement or ask a question, but rarely maintains the interaction even if asked a follow-up question. Ms. Garfield has noticed that Sandra will engage in reciprocal conversation with peers when the topic involves one of her preferred items or activities (e.g., anime, fashion, music). However, Sandra often speaks very quickly and at a high pitch during these conversations. In addition, she may clap her hands and shriek during the conversation.

Based on Ms. Garfield's observations, what social behaviors might she want to select as targets for Sandra? Table 3.3 provides examples of observed events and their connection to potential target social behaviors.

Selecting Settings and Materials

The setting and materials involved in PMLS are important because they set the occasion for interactions. Although peer mediation could occur anywhere, it is often optimal to begin with structured play or leisure settings because these situations tend to involve preferred items, are comfortable for the focal student and the peer, and require minimal demands outside of the social interactions. In addition, the teacher can provide high rates of support to the peer when the interaction is highly structured. Over time, this support can be faded and the structured play scenario can become gradually less structured. The interaction can then extend into general education classrooms and, eventually, less structured school environments such as hallways, playgrounds, and the lunchroom.

Table 3.3
Observed Events and Connection to Potential Target Behaviors

Event	Potential behaviors
Jen does most of the talking during interactions. Sandra engages in other activities (e.g., drawing).	• Reciprocal conversation • Attending to others when talking • Assertiveness during conversation
Sandra laughs though it does not appear to be related to discussion.	• Appropriate affective responding • Perspective taking
Sandra initiates with peers but does not respond to follow-up questions.	• Answering personal questions • Maintaining a conversation
Sandra engages in conversations pertaining to preferred items or activities, but talks quickly and at a high pitch. May also engage in hand-clapping and shrieking during conversation.	• Speaking clearly (pace and pitch) • Keeping hands down or using appropriate gestures

For preschool- and early elementary-aged children, structured play activities should involve materials that promote both parallel and interactive play, such as a sand table with corresponding toys, trains with tracks, LEGO®, and puzzles. These items set the occasion for simple though functional interactions such as exchanging materials and showing items to one another. As play skills progress, new materials and activities can be introduced based on student preference. For example, a PMLS session might involve interactions focused around a pretend play scenario with action figures or dolls.

As students progress in age or in ability to interact with others, it is important to implement PMLS in settings with less overall structure and with the materials that naturally occur in those settings. For example, students with DD may be taught to purchase preferred items at convenience stores by pairing them with typical peers who can model the component skills required to make a purchase (Blew, Schwartz, & Luce, 1985). PMLS can also be implemented during less structured periods of the school day, with transition between classes for middle and high school students being optimal social interaction times. The intervention could involve using peers to teach students with DD how to interact with others between classes, outside the lunchroom, or before or after school (Haring & Breen, 1992). The systematic progression of more to less structured settings is important so that the focal student can be successful during early sessions but still learn the range of environments in which social interaction must occur.

Teaching Peers to Interact With Young Children With DD

Peer training is often the most critical component of a successful PMLS. Peers may have limited knowledge of disabilities or awareness of children with DD (DiSalvo & Oswald, 2002). Thus, the first step in teaching peers to interact with children with DD is awareness training (Sperry et al., 2010), which could involve a discussion of similarities and differences among people along with a rationale for why it is important to teach individuals with DD to interact with their peers. For younger children it is important to make such a discussion as concrete as possible, with an emphasis on examples of behaviors.

After some basic discussion, it is important to role-play the procedures with peer-mediators so that they are able to practice the interactive skills and receive feedback prior to interacting with the focal student. The teacher can provide feedback to the peer regarding comments made and frequency of social interaction. Overall, the process should be enjoyable for the peers so that they are excited to begin their roles as peer mediators.

Following didactic instruction and role-play, peer mediators should receive explicit instruction in directing initiations toward and responding to the focal student with DD. This training should take place in a quiet area with only the teacher, peer mediators, and focal student in attendance. Instructors can provide models of the types of initiations and responses that peers need to learn to fully interact with the focal child. Peers can be taught to share ideas for playing with various items, and they should be taught how to provide praise to the focal child. Visual cues or video modeling can also be used to prepare peers for working with individuals with DD (Thiemann & Goldstein, 2001).

Teaching Peers to Interact With Adolescents With DD

Instructing peers to interact with students with DD in secondary settings requires additional consideration because social interactions become more complex and difficult to navigate for all adolescents, particularly those with social deficits (Carter & Kennedy, 2006). A primary consideration is the level of autonomy afforded students in secondary settings. Peers in secondary settings can often take on greater responsibility for organizing interactions earlier in the process than in primary grades. Bearing this in mind, it is helpful to remind peers to interact with the focal students similar to the way they would with their own friends, as opposed to how they might treat younger children (Hughes & Carter, 2008).

Activities can also vary at the secondary level. PMLS may involve students working together on class assignments (e.g., cooperative learning groups, offering corrective feedback) or facilitating and encouraging interactions with other classmates (e.g., making initial introductions, participating in extracurricular activities; Carter et al., 2008). The role of the teacher in these cases is that of a guide for the peers, and it may be important to discuss the balance between friendship and instruction that occurs during a peer-mediated partnership. Peers are certainly there to provide support and assistance, but they must always recognize and consider the new skills a focal student is capable of (Hughes & Carter, 2008). Authentic friendships have a greater chance of developing when students consider their role as a peer to be reinforcing, reciprocal, and enjoyable (Hughes & Carter, 2008).

Other considerations at the secondary level include confidentiality training, emergency preparation, and knowledge about how to handle issues pertaining to puberty. Because peers are more likely to learn about the disability of the focal student, it is important that they understand and commit to maintaining the confidentiality of any students with whom they are interacting. Increased autonomy can also lead to interactions that occur in settings with less adult supervision, thus creating the potential for peer mediators to be the first line of support if an emergency occurs (Carter et al., 2008). In case a paraprofessional or teacher is not readily accessible, peers should have basic training and review in school policies for fire, emergencies involving health concerns, and responding to accidents or violence. Last, peers need to be trained in how to handle sensitive scenarios that may arise as part of the transition to puberty for an individual with DD. Peers should be aware that focal students may develop a "crush" or sexual feelings toward the peer or other students and know to seek guidance as needed in responding appropriately to these situations. For example, if visual aids or verbal cues are being used to curtail an inappropriate behavior, the peer should be trained in their use. Peers should be taught that shaming or giving a lot of attention to an inappropriate behavior may actually increase the behavior. Instead it is best to remain calm, use correct and appropriate names when addressing the behavior, enlist the assistance of an available teacher or paraprofessional, and record what took place in order to share it with the teacher coordinating the PMLS program (Dubie, 2005).

A final domain unique to secondary students is that of transition planning. Many typically developing children engage in social interactions with one another around events that are likely to follow their time in high school. This can be a source of numerous target behaviors in the peer-mediated relationship and may also provide invaluable feedback for the student's teacher and parents by serving as an informal assessment of transition goals.

Preparing the Student With Developmental Disabilities

Despite the "peer mediation" terminology, individuals with DD may also require a range of supports from adult educators in order to successfully engage in PMLS. Many of these supports are provided during initial PMLS sessions (see following paragraphs), though it can be beneficial to prepare the focal student prior to implementation of the PMLS sessions. In essence, this is a preteaching step that gives the focal student the ability to predict the events that may occur with his or her peer.

Video modeling is one way to prepare a child with DD for the upcoming social interactions with peers during PMLS. For example, an instructor might show a video to a child with DD of two children interacting around a structured game and then instruct the focal child to perform the behaviors he or she observed in the video when interacting with his or her peer. Social narratives can also be helpful for students who read or comprehend more complex language. Social stories are one type of social narrative (see http://www.thegraycenter.org) and essentially provide a description of the interaction. Video modeling and social narratives offer a preview of events to come and may ease early instances of social interactions when PMLS are first implemented.

Administer Interaction Sessions

After all the preliminary components are completed, the easiest step of all may be to create the interaction sessions. When beginning the PMLS, the teacher should introduce the peer to the target student and remain in proximity for purposes of providing coaching and reinforcement to the peer. Sessions may be brief at this time (e.g., 5–8 min) to facilitate high rates of success and reduce the chance of boredom or lulls in the interaction. The teacher's role at this time is to provide prompts to the peer and deliver praise and other reinforcers to the peer and focal student as needed throughout the interaction. As the peer becomes increasingly confident and the focal student appears engaged, the teacher can increase session length and fade his or her level of involvement, allowing the peer to take over the intervention as intended.

Collecting Data

Regularly scheduled observations of PMLS sessions and recording of predetermined behaviors will provide insight into the quality and quantity of the peer's social guidance and the focal student's social engagement. Observation and data collection can provide information about when modifications, such as additional prompting or a pre-session social narrative, are needed for the focal student. Observation may also reveal other influences on social performance, such as peer errors or distractions in a particular classroom. The behaviors in Table 3.4 represent a sampling of social skills that could be recorded during observation sessions (English, Shafer, Goldstein, & Kaczmarek, 1997; Hughes & Carter, 2008).

Table 3.4
Behaviors to Record During Peer-Mediated Learning Strategies Sessions

Peer mediator behavior	Target student behaviors
Number of independent initiations	Responses to initiations of peer
Accurate delivery of reinforcers and/or praise	Initiations directed toward peer
Acceptable responses to initiations of target student	Instances of inappropriate behaviors
Asking for help as needed	

Figure 3.2 provides an example of an observation form that might be used to quickly identify whether the aforementioned behaviors are occurring. This could provide teachers with a way to quickly determine whether a change is necessary based on the observation of one or two PMLS sessions. A more detailed data collection instrument would be necessary for progress monitoring, wherein a teacher might assess for increases in frequency or percentage of correct responding over time.

Figure 3.2
Peer-Mediated Learning Strategies Observation Form

Peer Participant: _____ Target Student: _____				
Teacher: _____ Date: _____ Period: _____				
Location: _____ Activity: _____				
Key: N = never, S = seldom, O = often, A = always				
1. Peer is independently initiating activities with the target student	N	S	O	A
2. Target student is responding to peer initiations	N	S	O	A
3. Peer is using reinforcement effectively	N	S	O	A
4. Target student is initiating with peer	N	S	O	A
5. Peer is responding to the target student	N	S	O	A
6. Target student engages in inappropriate behaviors	N	S	O	A

Troubleshooting

After initial interactions are cultivated, the teacher's job is to conduct careful observation, collect and analyze data, and troubleshoot issues that may arise. In order to make effective modifications, it is critical to collect data on both peer and target student behavior. For example, if a peer asks a focal student a question but then quickly turns to converse with other peers in the class, then the peer will need additional coaching on effective social interactions with the target student. If data were not collected on the peer and target student, the teacher might fail to recognize that the poor responding by the focal student was actually related to the performance of the peer.

Another challenging scenario is when a focal student does not appear to enjoy a particular activity or item that was once a favorite. Conducting informal preference assessments of target students on a regular basis (every 2–3 weeks) can help because preferred items can change and vary over time. In some cases, this can be as simple as asking the focal student what items he or she enjoys playing with most or activities he or she wants to use with peers. For students with more severe impairments or who are nonverbal, teachers can place several preferred items out for the child to interact with and record items selected first or used most often (DeLeon & Iwata, 1996).

Ongoing Support for Peers

Ongoing support is a critical part of PMLS and ensures that peers receive coaching and assistance if challenges arise and as social skills goals are achieved. The type of ongoing support a teacher provides varies based on the age of the students. At the elementary level, the teacher should plan a time to model strategies and activities that have been observed as difficult for peers. As the peers gain confidence in conducting the intervention with the target students, involvement of the teacher or paraprofessional is faded (Carter & Hughes, 2007). For middle and high school students, weekly meetings designed for problem solving and discussion are a great way to provide ongoing support and allow peers to support one another in the process. Weekly meetings can also be a place to provide reinforcement for participation (e.g., verbal praise, certificates, letters home, occasional pizza parties, or other group social activities; Haring & Breen, 1992). The following format exemplifies a structured and orderly routine for a weekly meeting:

1. Conduct open discussion (involving special educator, teachers, and peers) of successes and challenges from the previous week's social interactions.

2. Discuss and make adjustments to the schedule, settings, materials, or types of interactions based on feedback from the peer.

3. Revisit, adapt, or add social skills for focal student to work on with peer.

4. Provide additional coaching, modeling, and reteaching of strategies as needed.

5. Probe peers to assess their opinions of the process.

6. Finish with praise for participating and a preferred activity.

Overcoming Communication Barriers

Although deficits in expressive communication can add to the complexity of peer-mediated interventions, communication deficits do not preclude PMLS. For example, researchers have used PMLS to increase the number of communicative behaviors emitted by nonvocal preschool children with autism during interactive play (Trembath, Balandin, Togher, & Stancliffe, 2009; Trottier, Kamp, & Mirenda, 2011). Interventionists can program words and phrases for focal children on a voice output communication aid (VOCA) and then train peers to interact with the focal students. Strategies to teach peers to interact when a child with DD uses a VOCA include illustrated stories to explain how the focal child communicates, direct instruction with role-play, and coaching during the interactive process. Similar to behaviors described previously, focal children can learn to request preferred items, respond to initiations of peers, and comment during games (e.g., "I almost had it that time") when using VOCAs as part of the interaction.

A unique aspect of preparing peers for PMLS with a VOCA is that the peers need an opportunity to interact with the VOCA in order to know how it works and how to model VOCA use for the focal child. Trembath and colleagues (2009) allowed peers to use the VOCA to interact with one another during the training process. The peers were then able to implement naturalistic teaching sessions with the focal child while also modeling use of the VOCA.

Final Thoughts

Peer-mediated learning strategies are beneficial for individuals with DD of all ages and across multiple settings (Sperry et al., 2010) and also benefit typical peers involved in the procedures (Hughes & Carter, 2008). Procedures can be modified for administration to individuals with more severe impairments, including co-occurring intellectual or language disabilities (e.g., Trembath et al., 2009). As such, PMLS can be incorporated into educational programs for almost all individuals with DD. We believe educators will find these interventions practical to implement and extremely powerful for all involved.

References

Bellini, S., Peters, J., Benner, L., & Hopf, A. (2007). A meta-analysis of school-based social skills interventions for children with autism spectrum disorders. *Remedial and Special Education, 28*,153–162. http://dx.doi.org/10.1177/07419325070280030401

Blew, P. A., Schwartz, I. S., & Luce, S. C. (1985). Teaching functional community skills to autistic children using nonhandicapped peer tutors. *Journal of Applied Behavior Analysis, 18*, 337–342. http://dx.doi.org/10.1901/jaba.1985.18-337

Carter, E. W., Cushing, L. S., & Kennedy, C. H. (2008). *Peer support strategies for improving all students' social lives and learning.* Baltimore, MD: Brookes.

Carter, E. W., & Hughes, C. (2007). Social interaction interventions: Promoting socially supportive environments and teaching new skills. In S. L. Odom, H. R. Horner, M. E. Snell, & J. B. Blacher (Eds.), *Handbook of developmental disabilities* (pp. 310–329). New York, NY: Guilford.

Carter, E. W., & Kennedy, C. H. (2006). Promoting access to the general curriculum using peer support strategies. *Research and Practice for Persons with Severe Disabilities, 31*, 284–292.

DeLeon, I. G., & Iwata, B. A. (1996). Evaluation of a multiple-stimulus presentation format for assessing reinforcer preferences. *Journal of Applied Behavior Analysis, 29*, 519–533. http://dx.doi.org/10.1901/jaba.1996.29-519

DiSalvo, C. A., & Oswald, D. P. (2002). Peer-mediated interventions to increase the social interaction of children with autism: Consideration of peer expectancies. *Focus on Autism and Other Developmental Disabilities, 17*, 198–207. http://dx.doi.org/10.1177/10883576020170040201

Dubie, M. (2005). Puberty. *The Reporter, 10*, 3–4.

English, K., Shafer, K., Goldstein, H., & Kaczmarek, L. (1997). *Teaching buddy skills to preschoolers.* Washington, DC: American Association on Mental Retardation.

Goldstein, H., Kaczmarek, L., Pennington, R., & Shafer, K. (1992). Peer-mediated intervention: Attending to, commenting on, and acknowledging the behavior of preschoolers with autism. *Journal of Applied Behavior Analysis, 25*, 289–305. http://dx.doi.org/10.1901/jaba.1992.25-289

Gresham, F. M., & Elliott, S. N. (2008). *Social Skills Improvement System – Rating Scales.* Minneapolis, MN: NCS Pearson.

Haring, T. G., & Breen, C. G. (1992). A peer-mediated social network intervention to enhance the social integration of persons with moderate and severe disabilities. *Journal of Applied Behavior Analysis, 25*, 319–334. http://dx.doi.org/10.1901/jaba.1992.25-319

Hughes, C., & Carter, E. W. (2008). *Peer buddy programs for successful secondary school inclusion.* Baltimore, MD: Brookes.

Kamps, D. M, Leonard, B. R., Vernon, S., Dugan, E. P., Delquadri, J. C., Gershon, B., …. Folk, L. (1992). Teaching social skills to students with autism to increase peer interactions in an integrated first-grade classroom. *Journal of Applied Behavior Analysis, 25*, 281–288. http://dx.doi.org/10.1901/jaba.1992.25-281

McConnell, S. R. (2002). Interventions to facilitate social interaction for young children with autism: Review of available research and recommendations for educational intervention and future research. *Journal of Autism and Developmental Disorders, 32*, 351–372. http://dx.doi.org/10.1023/A:1020537805154

Odom, S., Chandler, L., Ostrosky, M., McConnell, S., & Reaney, S. (1992). Fading teacher prompts from peer-initiation interventions for young children with disabilities. *Journal of Applied Behavior Analysis, 25*, 307–317. http://dx.doi.org/10.1901/jaba.1992.25-307

Odom, S. L., & Strain, P. S. (1986). A comparison of peer-initiation and teacher-antecedent interventions for promoting reciprocal social interactions of autistic preschoolers. *Journal of Applied Behavior Analysis, 19*, 58–72. http://dx.doi.org/10.1901/jaba.1986.19-59

Pierce, K., & Schreibman, L. (1995). Increasing complex social behaviors in children with autism: Effects of peer-implemented pivotal response training. *Journal of Applied Behavior Analysis, 28*, 285–295. http://dx.doi.org/10.1901/jaba.1995.28-285

Reichow, B., & Volkmar, F. R. (2010). Social skills interventions for individuals with autism: Evaluation for evidence-based practices within a best evidence synthesis framework. *Journal of Autism and Developmental Disorders, 40*, 149–166. http://dx.doi.org/10.1007/s10803-009-0842-0

Rogers, S. J. (2000). Interventions that facilitate socialization in children with autism. *Journal of Autism and Developmental Disorders, 30*, 399–409.

Sainato, D. M., Goldstein, H., & Strain, P. S. (1992). Effects of self-evaluation on preschool children's use of social interaction strategies with their classmates with autism. *Journal of Applied Behavior Analysis, 25*, 127–141. http://dx.doi.org/10.1901/jaba.1992.25-127

Sperry, L., Neitzel, J., & Engelhardt-Wells, K. (2010). Peer-mediated instruction and intervention strategies for students with autism spectrum disorders. *Preventing School Failure, 54*, 256–264. http://dx.doi.org/10.1080/10459881003800529

Thiemann, K., & Kamps, D. (2008). Promoting social communication competence of children with autism in integrated environments. In R. L. Simpson & B. S. Myles (Eds.), *Educating children and youth with autism* (pp. 267–298). Austin, TX: PRO-ED.

Thiemann, K. S., & Goldstein, H. (2001). Social stories, written text cues, and video feedback: Effects on social communication of children with autism. *Journal of Applied Behavior Analysis, 34*, 425–446. http://dx.doi.org/10.1901/jaba.2001.34-425

Thompson, S. M. (1996). Peer mediation: A peaceful solution. *School Counselor, 44*, 151–154.

Trembath, D., Balandin, S., Togher, L., & Stancliffe, R. J. (2009). Peer-mediated teaching and augmentative and alternative communication for preschool-aged children with autism. *Journal of Intellectual and Developmental Disability, 34*, 173-186. http://dx.doi.org/10.1080/13668250902845210

Trottier, N., Kamp, L., & Mirenda, P. (2011). Effects of peer-mediated instruction to teach use of speech-generating devices to students with autism in social game routines. *AAC: Augmentative and Alternative Communication, 27*, 26-39.

Chapter 4

Employing Teacher-Mediated Social Skills Strategies
Monica E. Delano and Liz Stone

The professional and lay literatures describe dozens of social skills interventions for children with autism spectrum disorder (ASD) or other developmental disabilities (DD). Researchers and practitioners often sort these interventions into a variety of categories, such as peer-mediated, adult-mediated, and comprehensive interventions. This chapter describes four teacher-mediated, child-focused social skills interventions. Similar to McConnell's descriptor, "child-specific interventions" (McConnell, 2002), the term "child-focused" in this context means that the interventions are designed to increase the social skills repertoire of a specific target child or of a small group of target children with ASD. These interventions generally involve an adult modeling, prompting, and reinforcing specific social behaviors in a natural or contrived context during initial training to provide children with multiple opportunities to respond, but peers must be included during the intervention process to ensure generalization. After introducing three vignettes that will be used throughout the chapter, four teacher-mediated strategies will be described: joint attention training, adult-mediated prompting and reinforcement, video modeling, and social skills group training.

Robert is 5 years old and has been enrolled in an early intervention preschool program since he was diagnosed with ASD at age 3½. He speaks in two word utterances and can request some preferred toys and edible items with prompting. He is fascinated by round objects (e.g., balls and wheels) and likes to play under a table and away from peers. He responds to adults' bids for joint attention inconsistently and rarely initiates joint attention.

Jalayla, a middle school student with ASD, has successfully learned many social skills (e.g., greeting familiar peers, ordering lunch in the cafeteria, requesting a break) from the video modeling tapes made by her teacher, Mr. Timbing. Jalayla's parents contacted Mr. Timbing for advice about how to help Jalayla participate more fully in the drama production at school. Mr. Timbing suggested that they use video modeling. After discussing the routines of daily practice sessions with the drama coach, her team decided that teaching Jalayla to greet her peers at the beginning of the practice sessions would be a good starting point. Individual students greet each other by saying things such as "What's up?" or "Good to see you." Usually, Jalayla arrives at the practice session and sits at the snack table without interacting with others.

Bradley is a ninth-grade student with intellectual disabilities in Mrs. Sockabee's resource class at Wannamaker High School. Bradley attends academic classes that are co-taught by a general education and special education teacher. Although Bradley is making adequate progress in his core classes, he struggles socially during transitions between classes as well as in the after-school band. He tells jokes repeatedly, stands too close to his communication partner, and talks loudly. Mrs. Sockabee and Bradley's mom agree that he needs additional instruction in social skills so that he can interact with his peers. Bradley and his mom and teacher set goals related to these skills. Bradley's mom notes that their family lives in a rural area in which he does not have many peer interactions outside the school day.

Strategy # 1: Joint Attention Training

What Is Joint Attention?

A father takes his young son for a walk in the zoo. As they pass the elephant cove, the child points to the elephants, says, "Elf" and looks at his father. The father looks at the elephants and says, "Yes, those are African elephants." The father and son proceed to have a conversation about the size and color of the elephants. They guess the length of the trunks and imagine what the elephants will have for dinner. The child's ability to draw his father's attention to something of interest created multiple opportunities for social interaction and learning. At the end of the day, the father and son sit on a bench and rest. The father gazes at the setting sun. The child follows his father's gaze and says, "Sun." The two then talk about the color of the sunset and where the sun will rise in the morning. In this case, the child's ability to follow his father's interest (the sun) subsequently led to additional opportunities for social interaction and learning.

The ability to coordinate attention between a communication partner and an object or event is called *joint attention* (Bakeman & Adamson, 1984; Wetherby, Prizant & Schuler, 2000). Joint attention consists of two classes of behavior: (a) responding to joint attention, in which a person responds to the eye-gaze shift or gesture of another person by attending to the same object, and (b) initiating joint attention, in which a person initiates a gesture or eye-gaze shift to coordinate attention with another person (Bruinsma, Koegel, & Koegel, 2004). Joint attention skills typically emerge during the first year and a half of life and serve as the foundation for the development of language and social skills (Bakeman & Adamson, 1984; Bruner, 1975; Whalen, Schreibman, & Ingersoll, 2006). Children with ASD demonstrate deficits in joint attention skills. Compared with typically developing children and children with other DD, children with ASD display fewer joint attention behaviors and initiate fewer bids for joint attention (Carpenter, Pennington, & Rogers, 2002; Charman et al., 2003; Loveland & Landry, 1986). This lack of joint attention skills limits interactions and decreases opportunities to learn through shared experiences with other communication partners (Adamson, Bakeman, Deckner, & Romski, 2009). In addition, research suggests that joint attention deficits are related to limitations in play, language acquisition, and the development of peer relationships (Prelock, Paul, & Allen, 2011). Joint attention, given the central role it plays in learning and social development, is considered a pivotal skill (Koegel & Koegel, 2006) and a priority treatment goal for young children with ASD (American Speech-Language-Hearing Association, ASHA, 2006; Prelock, 2006).

How to Implement Joint Attention Training

A growing body of evidence suggests that children with ASD can improve joint attention skills through the use of behavioral (e.g., prompting, shaping, reinforcement) and developmental (e.g., contingent imitation, expansion of language, following the child's lead) intervention strategies (see Prelock et al., 2011; White, 2011 for reviews). When beginning a joint attention training program, teachers must consider the child's current skills, identify target behaviors for initiating or responding to bids for joint attention (e.g., pointing, eye-gaze shifting, commenting), choose reinforcers, identify instructional procedures, and select a context for training. Much of the research on joint attention training has been conducted in the context of play (Meindl & Cannella-Malone, 2011). Because play is a natural context for young children, training in play situations may support generalization. Play also provides opportunities to incorporate preferred toys and engage various communication partners. Teachers must develop a plan to gradually fade prompts and return to natural reinforcement contingencies. Figure 4.1 provides a description of strategies Ms. Tallman, Robert's teacher, used to increase Robert's responses to and initiations of joint attention. Ms. Tallman based her instruction on a protocol designed by Taylor and Hoch (2008). Whereas joint attention training focuses on two classes of behaviors (initiating joint attention and responding to bids for joint attention), the remaining strategies may be used to teach a variety of responses.

Strategy # 2: Prompting and Reinforcement

What Is Prompting and Reinforcement?

Since the 1960s (Baer & Sherman, 1964) researchers have demonstrated the benefits of operant teaching techniques in educating children with disabilities. In fact, the science of applied behavior analysis serves as the foundation of the most effective interventions for individuals with ASD or other DD. Decades of research have shown that the use of prompting and reinforcement techniques is effective in teaching specific social skills (Banda & Hart, 2010; Charlop, Schreibman, & Thibodeau, 1985; Sarokoff, Taylor, & Poulson, 2001; Taylor & Harris, 1995), such as playing with toys (Ingenmey & Van Houten, 1991) and making conversation (Gena, Krantz, McClannahan, & Poulson, 1996; Taylor & Harris, 1995). Naturalistic prompting strategies, sometimes called *milieu teaching*, are especially useful for teaching social communication and language skills (Kaiser & Grim, 2006). The next section describes several naturalistic prompting procedures, including modeling, the mand-modeling procedure, and naturalistic time delay. These descriptions are based upon descriptions found in the practitioner literature (e.g. Collins, 2012; Kaiser & Grim, 2006; Webber & Scheuermann, 2008).

How to Implement the Modeling Procedure

The modeling procedure is very useful during acquisition when the student is learning a new word, sign, or symbol on an augmentative communication device (Kaiser & Grim, 2006). To implement the modeling procedure, the teacher starts by noting the student's interest in an object or activity, then establishes joint attention (Webber & Scheuermann, 2008). First, the teacher models a social

Figure 4.1
Joint Attention in Use

Target Behaviors: In response to Ms. Tallman's finger pointing, Robert will look at the target item, comment about the target item, and look back at Ms. Tallman.

Procedures

- Ms. Tallman points to the targeted item (e.g., ball) and says, "Look!"
- If Robert does not respond within 5 seconds, Ms. Tallman delivers a gestural prompt (e.g., points from child's visual orientation to the ball).
- If Robert still does not look in the direction of the ball, Ms. Tallman physically guides Robert to turn his head toward the ball.
- When Robert looks in the direction of the ball, Ms. Tallman provides an echoic prompt of a contextually appropriate comment (e.g., verbal model) for Robert to imitate, "It's flat."
- After making the comment, if Robert does not look back at Ms. Tallman within 2 seconds, she prompts Robert by moving her finger in an exaggerated fashion from the ball to her eyes.
- If Robert still does not look at her, Ms. Tallman provides a verbal prompt (e.g., "Look at the ball, then look back at me.")
- When Robert looks back at Ms. Tallman, she responds enthusiastically to his comment with an appropriate comment (e.g., "Yes, the ball is flat. It cannot bounce.") and a physical social interaction (e.g., high five).

Target Behaviors: Robert will point toward an item, make a directive statement (e.g., "look," "cool"), make a comment about the item, and look at Ms. Tallman.

Procedures

- Ms. Tallman walks Robert within two feet of a targeted item and waits 5 seconds to provide him with an opportunity to initiate a bid for joint attention.

- If Robert does not make a bid within 5 seconds, Ms. Tallman prompts him by guiding his hand to point to the item, provides an echoic prompt (e.g., "Say, 'Look!'"), and prompts him to look back at her.

- Ms. Tallman provides social comments and social reinforcement for each prompted response. (*Note*: Protacol per Talor & Hoch, 2008).

communicative behavior related to the student's interest. Then, the teacher waits several seconds to provide the student with an opportunity to imitate the model. Last, the teacher reinforces the student for imitating the model.

How to Implement the Mand-Modeling Procedure

The mand-modeling procedure requires students to move beyond simple imitation of social communicative behaviors. As with the modeling procedure, the teacher notes the student's interest in an object or activity and establishes joint attention (Webber & Scheuermann, 2008). Then the teacher provides a request (called a *mand*; e.g., "Choose one") and gives the student an opportunity to respond. If the student provides a correct response, the teacher reinforces the student (e.g., praise and access to the desired object). If the student makes an error or does not respond, the teacher repeats the mand and provides a model. The teacher reinforces the student for imitating the model.

How to Implement Naturalistic Time Delay

Naturalistic time delay is useful for teaching initiation (Kaiser & Grimm, 2006). The teacher establishes joint attention and interrupts an ongoing routine. Then the teacher looks at the student expectantly and waits a set interval (e.g., 5 s) for the student to make a response. The teacher reinforces the student for a correct response (e.g., praise and continuation of routine). If the student does not make a correct response, the teacher can implement the mand-model or model procedure (Webber & Scheuermann, 2008).

> *Ms. Tallman implemented naturalistic time delay to teach Robert to initiate requests. She identified several preferred play routines and implemented instruction during these routines. For example, Robert loves getting pushed on the swing at the playground. Ms. Tallman starts pushing Robert on the swing at the start of recess. After a few pushes, she stops and looks expectantly at Robert. Robert says, "Push please." Ms. Tallman replies, "Good asking. You want a big push." Ms. Tallman pushes the swing and Robert laughs happily.*

These naturalistic prompting procedures provide effective methods to teach gradually more complex social communicative behavior during typical daily activities.

Strategy #3: Video Modeling

What Is Video Modeling?

Video modeling involves a student repeatedly watching a video of another individual correctly performing a targeted skill. After viewing the video, the learner has an opportunity to perform the targeted skill in a natural setting. Video modeling may be a good match for some learners with ASD or other DD because video clips can focus the learner's attention on salient aspects of a task, and watching videos may be a preferred activity for children. Video modeling has been demonstrated to be effective in teaching a wide range of self-help, academic, community, and social skills (Ayres and Langone, 2005; Hammond, Muething, Ayres, & Gast, 2010). In particular, video modeling has been demonstrated to increase spontaneous requesting (Wert & Neisworth, 2003), social initiations (Buggey, 2005; Nikopoulos & Keenan, 2004), social interactions (Sansosti & Powell-Smith, 2008), compliment giving (Apple, Billingsley, & Schwartz, 2005), and play (D'Ateno, Mangiapanello, & Taylor, 2003; MacDonald, Clark, Garrigan, & Vangala, 2005; Nikopoulos & Keenan, 2003, 2007; Taylor, Leven, & Jasper, 1999). Video modeling, used alone or in combination with other interventions, is an effective strategy for teaching social skills to children and youth with ASD or other DD. There are four basic types of video modeling procedures (Cox, Delano, Sturgill, Fanzone, & Collet-Klinberg, 2009; see Table 4.1 for descriptions)

Table 4.1
Types of Video Modeling

Method	Description
Basic video modeling	Adult or peer is filmed performing the skill. Student watches video.
Video self-modeling	Positive self review: Students watch video of themselves performing skill. Video film forward: Students watch edited video to see themselves performing skill as they will in the future (Buggey, 2009).
Point-of-view video modeling	Video is taken from perspective of learner; students see exactly what they would see if they performed the skill.
Video prompting	Student performs each step in a chained task immediately after watching a video in which a model performs the task.

How to Implement Video Modeling

Implementing one of the four video modeling procedures may at first seem like a daunting task. However, given recent advances in video technology, making videos and implementing video modeling is relatively easy after a little practice. Delano, Whalon, and Wert (2013) discussed the important steps for implementation of video modeling. The steps may be divided into three stages: planning for intervention, creating the video, and implementing the video modeling. The most important steps in each stage are highlighted here.

When planning to implement the video modeling procedure, several steps should be followed:

1. Identify the target skill in precise, measurable terms.
2. Develop a data collection procedure to collect data.

3. Determine which type of video modeling will be used to teach the target skill and obtain the necessary equipment.

4. Obtain permission from parents and guardians to film students.

5. Identify the settings for videotaping, as well as settings in which the student will be observed to ensure generalization of the skills.

6. Determine a schedule and procedure for viewing the video and collection of data.

7. Identify how to ensure generalization across people, activities and settings.

It is important to note that research does not provide guidance regarding the best type of video modeling for specific students or tasks. Practitioners will need to base their selection on the nature of the target skill and experience with particular students. The following steps are required to create the video:

1. Write a script or task analysis for the video.

2. Determine a method to capture the target behavior (e.g., role play, imitation, or natural clips).

3. Train the models or actors.

4. Videotape the models (actors) and the target student.

5. Edit the video for final presentation to the target student.

Last, implementation of the video modeling strategy includes five steps:

1. Show the final video to the student on the predetermined schedule.

2. Collect data on the student's behavior during video viewing (e.g., attending behavior).

3. Collect intervention data on the student's use of the target behavior.

4. Make data-based instructional modifications as needed.

5. Fade the video and follow the plan for generalization and maintenance.

After talking with her coach about making a video at practice, Jalayla agreed to set a goal to greet three different people before getting an after school snack. Mr. Timbing suggested they use basic video modeling. Jalayla's coach wrote a short script for video, and Jalayla's sister played Jalayla's role. The tape illustrated Jalayla's sister greeting three different people by going to them, standing close to them, making eye contact, and saying "What's up?" Jalayla watched the tape prior to each practice session. After several weeks, her coach reported that Jalayla began greeting others appropriately and sometimes exceeded her goal of three greetings. In addition, her parents noticed that Jalayla greeted family members at a reunion the next weekend.

Strategy #4: Social Skills Training Groups

What Are Social Skills Training Groups?

According to Ferraioli and Harris (2011), there are two essential components of social competence. First, individuals must use distinct social skills that can be employed in many different situations. For example, effective social interactions require the ability to display specific skills such as greeting others, monitoring voice level, and establishing eye contact in the appropriate social context. In these groups, clinicians or educators use direct instruction or cognitive behavioral strategies to increase social behavior skills of school-aged children with ASD and other disabilities (see reviews by Bellini, Peters, Benner, & Hopf, 2007; Cappadocia & Weiss, 2011; Rao, Beidel, & Murray, 2008; and Reichow & Volkmar, 2010).

The second essential component of social effectiveness involves social cognition and the interpretation of social cues (Ferraioli & Harris, 2011). That is, students learn to make inferences about others' social behaviors based on facial expression, body movements, and tone of voice. Interventionists have used social skills training groups to improve the social cognition (awareness) skills of children with ASD, including "theory of mind." (Baron-Cohen, 1989), which includes the ability to take another person's perspective. Studies by Ozonoff and Miller (1995), Solomon, Goodlin-Jones, & Anders (2004), and Turner-Brown, Perry, Dichter, Bodfish, and Penn (2008) used various treatment packages to investigate improvements in social cognitive skills.

Research studies have included a variety of strategies to teach social awareness in social skills group training, including role-play, watching video tapes, modeling facial expressions, and using a modified version of the Social Cognition and Interaction Training program (SCIT; Roberts, Penn, & Combs, 2004). SCIT activities use videotapes in which subjects identify scenarios related to facial recognition of interest or disinterest and relevant facts or irrelevant facts. Overall, results of these interventions were mixed. For example, Ozonoff and Miller (1995) described "meaningful changes" in skills related to false belief tasks, but teachers and parents did not observe improvements in general social competence. These results suggest that improving theory of mind skills does not necessarily lead to observable improvements in social functioning. Research subjects in Solomon and colleagues' (2004) study showed varying degrees of improvement on measures of facial recognition, theory of mind, and depression. Turner-Brown and colleagues (2008) found gradual improvements in social awareness using SCIT activities but did not show improvements in the way subjects behaved or interacted with others. Thus, social skills training groups have been used to teach social skills and social cognition to individuals with ASD or other DD.

How to Implement Group Social Skill Training

To be effective, social skills groups must be carefully planned, use systematic instruction, and evaluate effects of instruction on an ongoing basis (Sansosti, Powell-Smith, & Cowan, 2010). Prior to instruction within a social skills group, facilitators should determine which students (including typically developing peers) and skills will be included in the treatment package. Webb, Miller, Pierce, Strawser, and Jones (2004) and White (2011) suggested using the present level of performance from students' individualized education programs to identify target skills. Typically developing peers are included to model social skills correctly. Also, facilitators should decide if a classroom management or reinforcement system should be included (see Kamps, Leonard, Vernon, Dugan, & Delquadri, 1992) and what type of treatment schedule will produce the most effective results. Groups that include students with ASD and intellectual disabilities may benefit from more frequent instructional sessions. Last, facilitators choose the settings for instruction as well as the environments in which the students will be evaluated for generalization skills (Tse, Strulovitch, Tagalakis, Meng, & Fombonne, 2007).

Group facilitators may choose to use a general teaching protocol similar to a study by White (2011). White divided instructional sessions into five components. First, facilitators and students review skills taught in previous sessions. White also emphasized the importance of having students "buy into" the instructional program. Next, facilitators present the new target skill and discuss when and where the skill may be used. Third, students practice the new skill using role-plays, modeling, and a variety of other techniques (Kroeger, Schultz, & Newsom, 2007; Webb et al., 2004). Fourth, students review the new skills and the steps for implementation. Last, facilitators support students as they develop goals for the use of new skills in other settings.

Following instructional sessions, facilitators collect observational data on student performance, including data related to students' use of target skills in naturalistic environments. After analyzing student performance data, facilitators (and possibly the students themselves) make instructional decisions, such as whether additional time or instruction is necessary to master the target skills. If the target goals have not been met, consider other instructional techniques (e.g., direct instruction, systematic prompting) to reinforce the instruction. Last, facilitators plan for additional steps, including communication with trainers and distribution of additional data sheets to ensure generalization of skills to novel situations. Perhaps most importantly, students and interested parties must celebrate goal achievement.

The team determines that a social skills training group would be the best instructional setting for Bradley to learn these skills. Bradley attends a social skills group two times per week with other students who also struggle with social skills. Mrs. Sockabee leads the group. During group time, participants decide which skills to practice, role-play the skills, and evaluate their use of the skills in the small group. Mrs. Sockabee also sends out surveys every week to other teachers and the students' families to determine whether they observe Bradley and his peers using the skills that the group practices. Mrs. Sockabee also tells the observers what steps the students will use to demonstrate use of the new skills. For example, Mrs. Sockabee notes on the survey that if a student is greeting a peer, the student should be standing an appropriate distance from the communication partner. Every 2 weeks, Bradley and the others in the group look at the results of the surveys and discuss whether they have met their goals. During one particular week, Bradley set the goal of standing at an appropriate distance with six different individuals during conversations. When he looked at the surveys at the end of 2 weeks, he realized that seven different people observed him standing at an appropriate distance. Because he exceeded his goal, Bradley chose to work next on choosing appropriate subjects to talk about, rather than telling jokes repeatedly. Bradley continued to make goals and track his progress throughout his ninth grade at Wannamaker High.

Final Thoughts

Teacher-mediated interventions play important roles in social skills programming. Joint attention training is a critical component of early intervention programming for young children with ASD. Prompting and reinforcement techniques enable instructors to provide students with multiple opportunities to respond and receive reinforcement while gradually transferring stimulus control from prompts to natural antecedents. Video modeling is effective in teaching a wide variety of skills. Last, social skills training groups show promise in improving social skills.

References

Adamson, L. B., Bakeman, R., Deckner, D. F., & Romski, M. (2009). Joint engagement and the emergence of language in children with autism and Down syndrome. *Journal of Autism and Developmental Disorders, 39*, 84–96. http://dx.doi.org/10.1007/s10803-008-0601-7

American Speech-Language-Hearing Association (ASHA). (2006). *Roles and responsibilities of Speech-Language Pathologists in diagnosis, assessment and treatment of autism spectrum disorders across the life span* [Position Statement]. Retrieved from http://www.asha.org/policy

Apple, A. L., Billingsley, F., & Schwartz, I. S. (2005). Effects of video modeling alone and with self-management on compliment-giving behaviors of children with high-functioning ASD. *Journal of Positive Behavior Interventions, 7*, 33–46. http://dx.doi.org/10.1177/10983007050070010401

Ayres, K., & Langone, J. (2005). Intervention and instruction with video for students with autism: A review of the literature. *Education and Training in Developmental Disabilities, 40*, 183–196.

Baer, D. M., & Sherman, J. A. (1964). Reinforcement control of generalized imitation in young children. *Journal of Experimental Child Psychology, 1*, 37–49. http://dx.doi.org/10.1016/0022-0965(64)90005-0

Bakeman, R., & Adamson, L. B. (1984). Coordinating attention to people and objects in mother-infant and peer-infant interaction. *Child Development, 55*, 1278–1289. http://dx.doi.org/10.2307/1129997

Banda, D., & Hart, S. (2010). Increasing peer-to-peer social skills through direct instruction of two elementary school girls with autism. *Journal of Research in Special Education Needs, 10*, 124–132. http://dx.doi.org/10.1111/j.1471-3802.2010.01149.x

Baron-Cohen, S. (1989). The autistic child's theory of mind: A case of specific developmental delay. *Journal of Child Psychology and Psychiatry, 30*, 285–298. http://dx.doi.org/10.1111/j.1469-7610.1989.tb00241.x

Bellini, S., Peters, J. K., Benner, L., & Hopf, A. (2007). A meta-analysis of school-based social skills interventions for children with autism spectrum disorders. *Remedial and Special Education, 28*, 153–162. http://dx.doi.org/10.1177/07419325070280030401

Bruinsma, Y., Koegel, R. L., & Koegel, L. K. (2004). Joint attention and children with autism: A review of the literature. *Mental Retardation and Developmental Disabilities Research Reviews, 10*, 169–175. http://dx.doi.org/10.1002/mrdd.20036

Bruner, J. (1975). From communication to language: A psychological perspective. *Cognition, 3,* 255–287. http://dx.doi.org/10.1016/0010-0277(74)90012-2

Buggey, T. (2005). Video modeling applications with students with autism spectrum disorder in a small private school setting. *Focus on Autism and Other Developmental Disabilities, 20,* 52–63. http://dx.doi.org/10.1177/10883576050200010501

Buggey, T. (2009). *Seeing is believing: Video self-modeling for people with autism and other developmental disabilities.* Bethesda, MD: Woodbine House.

Cappadocia, C., & Weiss, J. (2011). Review of social skills training groups for youth with Asperger syndrome and high functioning autism. *Research in Autism Spectrum Disorders, 5,* 70–78. http://dx.doi.org/10.1016/j.rasd.2010.04.001

Carpenter, T., Pennington, B. F., & Rogers, S. J. (2002). Interrelations among social-cognitive skills in young children with autism. *Journal of Autism and Developmental Disorders, 32,* 91–106.

Charlop, M. H., Schreibman, L., & Thibodeau, M. G. (1985). Increasing spontaneous verbal responding in autistic children using a time delay procedure. *Journal of Applied Behavior Analysis, 18,* 155–166. http://dx.doi.org/10.1901/jaba.1985.18-155

Charman, T., Baren-Cohen, S., Swettenham, J., Baird, G., Drew, A., & Cox, A. (2003). Predicting language outcome in infants with autism and pervasive and developmental disorder. *International Journal of Language & Communication Disorders, 38,* 265–285. http://dx.doi.org/10.1080/136820310000104830

Collins, B. C. (2012). *Systematic instruction for students with moderate and severe disabilities.* Baltimore, MD: Brookes.

Cox, A. W., Delano, M. E., Sturgill, T. R., Franzone, E., & Collet-Klinberg, L. (2009). *Video modeling–training materials.* Chapel Hill, NC: National Professional Development Center on Autism Spectrum Disorders, Frank Porter Graham Child Development Institute, University of North Carolina.

D'Ateno, P., Mangiapanello, K., & Taylor, B. (2003). Using video modeling to teach complex play sequences to a preschooler with autism. *Journal of Positive Behavior Interventions, 5,* 5–11. http://dx.doi.org/10.1177/10983007030050010801

Delano, M. E., & Whalon, K., & Wert, B. Y. (2013). Increasing social skills. In D. E. Perner & M. E. Delano (Eds.), *A guide to teaching students with autism spectrum disorders.* Arlington, VA: Council for Exceptional Children.

Ferraioli, S. J., & Harris, S. L. (2011). Effective educational inclusion of students on the autism spectrum. *Journal of Contemporary Psychotherapy, 41,* 19–28. http://dx.doi.org/10.1007/s10879-010-9156-y

Gena, A., Krantz, P. J., McClannahan, L. E., & Poulson, C. L. (1996). Training and generalization of affective behavior displayed by youth with autism. *Journal of Applied Behavior Analysis, 29,* 291–304. http://dx.doi.org/10.1901/jaba.1996.29-291

Hammond, D. L., Muething, C. M., Ayres, K. M., & Gast, D. L. (2010). Effectiveness of video modeling to teach iPod use to students with moderate intellectual disabilities. *Education and Training in Autism and Developmental Disabilities, 45,* 525–538.

Ingenmey, R., & Van Houten, R. (1991). Using time delay to promote spontaneous speech in an autistic child. *Journal of Applied Behavior Analysis, 25,* 591–596. http://dx.doi.org/10.1901/jaba.1991.24-591

Kaiser, A. P., & Grim, J. C. (2006). Teaching functional communication skills. In M. E. Snell & F. Brown (Eds.), *Instruction of students with severe disabilities* (6th ed., pp. 447–488). Upper Saddle River, NJ: Pearson.

Kamps, D. M., Leonard, B. R., Vernon, S., Dugan, E. P., & Delquadri, J. (1992). Teaching social skills to students with autism to increase peer interactions in an integrated first grade classroom. *Journal of Applied Behavior Analysis, 25,* 281–288. http://dx.doi.org/10.1901/jaba.1992.25-281

Koegel, R. L., & Koegel, L. K. (2006). *Pivotal response treatments for autism: Communication, social and academic development.* Baltimore, MD: Brookes.

Kroeger, K. A., Schultz, J. R., & Newsom, C. (2007). A comparison of two group-delivered social skills programs for young children with autism. *Journal of Autism and Developmental Disorders, 37,* 808–817. http://dx.doi.org/10.1007/s10803-006-0207-x

Loveland, K. A., & Landry, S. H. (1986). Joint attention and language in autism and developmental language delay. *Journal of Autism and Developmental Disorders, 16,* 335–349. http://dx.doi.org/10.1007/bf01531663

MacDonald, R., Clark, M., Garrigan, M., & Vangala, M. (2005). Using video modeling to teach pretend play to children with autism. *Behavioral Interventions, 20,* 225–238. http://dx.doi.org/10.1002/bin.197

McConnell, S. (2002). Interventions to facilitate social interactions for young children with autism: Review of available research and recommendations for educational intervention and future research. *Journal of Autism and Developmental Disorders, 32,* 351–372.

Meindl, J. N., & Cannella-Malone, H. I. (2011). Initiating and responding to joint attention bids in children with autism: A review of the literature. *Research in Developmental Disabilities, 32,* 1441–1454. http://dx.doi.org/10.1016/j.ridd.2011.02.013

Nikopoulos, C. K., & Keenan, M. (2003). Promoting social initiation in children with autism using video modeling. *Behavioral Interventions, 18,* 87–108. http://dx.doi.org/10.1002/bin.129

Nikopoulos, C. K., & Keenan, M. (2004). Effects of video modeling on social initiations by children with autism. *Journal of Applied Behavior Analysis, 37,* 93–96. http://dx.doi.org/10.1901/jaba.2004.37-93

Nikopoulos, C. K., & Keenan, M. (2007). Using video modeling to teach complex social sequences to children with autism. *Journal of Autism and Developmental Disorders, 37,* 678–693. http://dx.doi.org/10.1007/s10803-006-0195-x

Ozonoff, S., & Miller, J. N. (1995). Teaching theory of mind: A new approach to social skills training for individuals with autism. *Journal of Autism and Developmental Disorders, 25,* 415–433. http://dx.doi.org/10.1007/bf02179376

Prelock, P. A. (2006). *Autism spectrum disorders: Issues in assessment and intervention.* Austin, TX: Pro-Ed.

Prelock, P. A., Paul, R., & Allen, E. M. (2011). Evidence-based treatments in communication for children with autism spectrum disorders. In B. Reichow, P. Doehring, D. Cicchetti, & F. Volkmar (Eds.), *Evidence-based practices and treatments for children with autism*. New York, NY: Springer.

Rao, P. A., Beidel, D. C., & Murray, M. J. (2008). Social skills interventions for children with Asperger's syndrome or high-functioning autism: A review and recommendations. *Journal of Autism and Developmental Disorders, 38*, 353–361. http://dx.doi.org/10.1007/s10803-007-0402-4

Reichow, B., & Volkmar, F. (2010). Social skills interventions for individuals with autism: Evaluation for evidence-based practices within a best evidence synthesis framework. *Journal of Autism and Developmental Disorders, 40*, 149–166. http://dx.doi.org/10.1007/s10803-009-0842-0

Roberts, D. L., Penn, D., & Combs, D. R. (2004). *Social cognition and interaction training*. Unpublished treatment manual.

Sansosti, F. J., & Powell-Smith, K. A. (2008). Using computer-presented social stories and video models to increase the social communication skills of children with high-functioning autism spectrum disorders. *Journal of Positive Behavior Interventions, 10*, 162–178. http://dx.doi.org/10.1177/1098300708316259

Sansosti, F. J., Powell-Smith, K. A., & Cowan, R. J. (2010). *High-functioning autism/Asperger syndrome in schools: Assessment and intervention*. New York, NY: Guilford.

Sarokoff, R. A., Taylor, B. A., & Poulson, C. L. (2001). Teaching children with autism to engage in conversational exchanges: Script fading with embedded textual stimuli. *Journal of Applied Behavior Analysis, 34*, 81–84. http://dx.doi.org/10.1901/jaba.2001.34-81

Solomon, M., Goodlin-Jones, B. L., & Anders, T. F. (2004). A social adjustment enhancement intervention for high functioning autism, Asperger's syndrome, and pervasive developmental disorder NOS. *Journal of Autism and Developmental Disorders, 34*, 649–668. http://dx.doi.org/10.1007/s10803-004-5286-y

Taylor, B., Leven, L., & Jasper, S. (1999). Increasing play related statements in children with autism toward their siblings: Effects of video modeling. *Journal of Developmental and Physical Disabilities, 11*, 253–264.

Taylor, B. A., & Harris, S. L. (1995). Teaching children with autism to seek information: Acquisition of novel information and generalization of responding. *Journal of Applied Behavior Analysis, 28*, 3–14. http://dx.doi.org/10.1901/jaba.1995.28-3

Taylor, B. A., & Hoch, H. (2008). Teaching children with autism to respond to and initiate bids for joint attention. *Journal of Applied Behavior Analysis, 41*, 377–391. http://dx.doi.org/10.1901/jaba.2008.41-377

Tse, J., Strulovitch, J., Tagalakis, V., Meng, L., & Fombonne, E. (2007). Social skills training for adolescents with Asperger syndrome and high functioning autism. *Journal of Autism and Developmental Disorders, 37*, 1960–1968. http://dx.doi.org/10.1007/s10803-006-0343-3

Turner-Brown, L. M., Perry, T. D., Dichter, G. S., Bodfish, J. W., & Penn, D. L. (2008). Brief report: Feasibility of social cognition and interaction training for adults with high functioning autism.

Journal of Autism and Developmental Disorders, 38, 1777–1784. http://dx.doi.org/10.1007/s10803-008-0545-y

Webb, B. J., Miller, S., Pierce, T. B., Strawser, S., & Jones, W. P. (2004). Effects of social skill instruction for high-functioning adolescents with autism spectrum disorders. *Focus on Autism and Other Developmental Disabilities, 19,* 53–62. http://dx.doi.org/10.1177/10883576040190010701

Webber, J., & Scheuermann, B. K. (2008). *Educating students with autism: A quick start manual.* Austin, TX: PRO-ED.

Wert, B. Y., & Neisworth, J. T. (2003). Effects of video self-modeling on spontaneous requesting in children with autism. *Journal of Positive Behavior Interventions, 5,* 30–34. http://dx.doi.org/10.1177/10983007030050010501

Wetherby, A. M., Prizant, B. M., & Schuler, A. L. (2000). Understanding the nature of communication and language impairments. In A. M. Wetherby & B. M. Prizant (Eds.), *Autism spectrum disorders: A transactional developmental perspective* (pp. 109–141). Baltimore, MD: Brookes.

Whalen, C., Schreibman, L., & Ingersoll, B. (2006). The collateral effects of joint attention training on social initiations, positive affect, imitation, and spontaneous speech for children with autism. *Journal of Autism and Developmental Disorders, 36,* 655–664. http://dx.doi.org/10.1007/s10803-006-0108-z

White, S. W. (2011). *Social skills training for children with Asperger syndrome and high-functioning autism.* New York, NY: Guilford.

Chapter 5

Using Embedded Instruction to Enhance Social-Emotional Skills
Tara McLaughlin and Patricia Snyder

Most children in Ms. Roberts' preschool classroom are able to follow the daily schedule, participate in routines and activities, and play well with their peers. A few children in her classroom need extra help to play, be part of a group, and make friends. Ms. Roberts wants to identify strategies for teaching social-emotional skills for two children in her classroom: Sue and Damien. Sue is a 4-year-old diagnosed with Down syndrome. She uses a few single words and signs to express her wants and needs but does not interact with other children in the classroom. Damien is 4 1/2-years old and exhibits developmental delays. Damien is able to express his wants and needs using short phrases, but he does not interact or play with his peers and during free-play spends most of his time lying on the floor pushing a truck back and forth.

Developing or strengthening children's social and emotional competence has been identified as an important curricular focus in contemporary preschool programs, especially in programs that include young children at risk for learning and behavioral challenges or those with disabilities. Developmental and behavioral scientists generally view social-emotional competence as a multivariate construct (Denham, 2006; Domitrovich, Cortes, & Greenberg, 2007; Fantuzzo, Bulotsky-Shearer, Fusco, & McWayne, 2005; Odom, McConnell, & Brown, 2008; Vaughn et al., 2003). Examples of knowledge and skills associated with this multivariate construct include social competencies (e.g., understanding social cues, social problem solving); emotional competencies (e.g., emotion knowledge and expression, empathy and perspective taking); and, in some cases, self-regulation and executive functions (e.g., attention and impulse control, planning skills).

Although consensus exists about the importance of developing or strengthening young children's social-emotional competence, there is less agreement about related knowledge and skills that should be targeted for intervention or instruction. Recent conceptualizations from a social-emotional learning perspective, however, are useful for (a) identifying social, emotional, and self-regulatory or executive function skills needed to strengthen the social-emotional competence of young children at risk or those with identified disabilities; and (b) optimizing early learning experiences through promotion, prevention, and intervention strategies that will support preschool children to learn and use these skills (Dodge, 2011). In addition, because social-emotional learning and approaches to learning are two critical domains of school readiness identified by the National Education Goals Panel (1996), most states have included competencies or skills related to social and emotional learning as well as approaches to learning in their early learning guidelines or foundations (Connors-Tadros, 2013). Examples include self-awareness, self-regulation, and self-esteem; identifying and expressing emotions, responding to others' emotions, and showing empathy; engaging in appropriate interactions with adults and peers; joining in group activities; cooperating and engaging in play with others; understanding and following social rules; engaging in social problem-solving; and forming close relationships and friendships with other children.

To support and strengthen young children's social-emotional competence, teachers create learning environments that are nurturing and responsive to children's needs, engage children in high-quality activities to help them learn and practice social and emotional skills, and promote positive interactions with adults and peers. The preschool curriculum should include sufficient and intentional learning opportunities for all young children to learn and use social-emotional skills. In addition, children like Sue and Damien benefit from additional learning opportunities and explicit teaching to learn and use skills necessary to navigate the social environment in the preschool classroom, express their emotions in appropriate ways, and make and maintain lasting friendships. Ms. Roberts needs strategies that will help her provide these additional learning opportunities and explicit teaching within and across activities, routines, and transitions in her preschool classroom.

Several teachers have given Ms. Roberts ideas about ways to strengthen Sue and Damien's social-emotional competence. The therapists on the team suggested that they could work with Sue and Damien one-on-one each day to give them targeted practice on some essential skills. Ms. Roberts' appreciates their help, but she would like to try to embed Sue's and Damien's instruction during the ongoing activities, routines, and transitions in her classroom.

Embedded instruction is an evidence-informed, multicomponent approach to intentional and systematic instruction that occurs during everyday activities, routines, and transitions. It focuses on what to teach (specifying the instructional content to be taught); when to teach (identifying when this content should be taught); how to teach (using intentional and systematic instructional procedures to teach specified content); and how to evaluate (evaluating whether instruction is implemented as planned and results in child learning as part of data-based decision making; Snyder, Hemmeter, Sandall, McLean, & McLaughlin, 2013). This approach to intentional instruction is distinguished by an emphasis on providing learning opportunities that are embedded rather than decontextualized and is based on principles related to general case programming and differentiated instruction (e.g., Horner, 2005; Snell, 2007).

In this chapter, we briefly describe the background and empirical evidence for embedded instruction, the major components of embedded instruction, and the practices associated with each component. We illustrate how the components and associated practices could be used by Ms. Roberts to develop or strengthen targeted skills related to social-emotional competence for Sue and Damien.

Implementing Embedded Instruction

Background and Empirical Evidence Related to Embedded Instruction

The concept of embedding instruction had been described as part of several approaches to support children's learning, including incidental teaching (Hart & Risley, 1974, 1975), naturalistic teaching (Rule, Losardo, Dinnebeil, Kaiser, & Rowland, 1998), activity-based instruction (Bricker & Cripe, 1992; Losardo & Bricker, 1994), embedded instruction (Horn & Banerjee, 2009; McDonnell, Johnson, & McQuivey, 2008; Snyder et al., 2013), and transition-based teaching (Werts, Wolery, Holcombe-Ligon, Vassilaros, & Billings, 1992). Despite different labels, several common features have been identified across these various approaches. First, the contexts for instruction are children's typically occurring activities, routines, transitions, or everyday learning experiences. Second, the content of instruction focuses on behaviors or skills needed by the child to meet activity demands or characteristics, participate in typically occurring activities and routines, or achieve desired child developmental or learning outcomes. Third, each instructional episode is typically child-initiated or initiated by an adult based on the child's focus of attention or interest, and a natural or logically planned consequence follows the child's response. Fourth, the adults who implement the instruction are those who interact regularly with the child (Snyder et al., 2014).

Despite identified similarities, two different approaches have been described using the term embedded instruction. The first approach focuses on embedding *into* ongoing activities, routines, or transitions and has been more commonly used with young children (ages 3–8). The second interpretation focuses on embedding *between* activities or routines (or during transitions) and has been more commonly used with older children (ages 8–18).

In the first approach, instruction for children on one or more targeted skills occurs within ongoing activities or routines in the classroom without significantly altering or disrupting the flow of the activity or routine. As part of this approach, the instruction provided is focused on a targeted skill or cluster of skills that can be logically incorporated within a naturally occurring activity or routine in the classroom. Instruction on the same targeted skill or cluster of skills can occur in more than one activity or routine across the preschool day. In this approach, teachers ensure intentional instruction on selected skills that increase participation or improve skills related to an activity or routine. For example, Ms. Roberts might teach Sue new signs for toys when she is playing in a center and new signs for food during snack time. As Sue reaches for new toys during center time or food during snack time, Ms. Roberts names the item, models the sign, and helps Sue make the sign. Learning new signs during the center activity and snack routine helps Sue learn new vocabulary so she can request toys or food from her peers and teachers while playing or eating. (For more examples and research involving this approach to embedded instruction, see Fox & Hanline, 1993; Grisham-Brown, Pretti-Frontczak, Hawkins, & Winchell, 2009; Grisham-Brown, Schuster, Hemmeter, & Collins, 2000; Malmskog & McDonnell, 1999; McBride & Schwartz, 2003; Schepis, Reid, Ownbey, & Parsons, 2001; Snyder et al., 2011; Venn et al.,1993.)

In the second approach, embedded instruction is a strategy to teach skills between ongoing activities or routines in the classroom. Instruction occurs during natural breaks in activities or during transitions between activities. As part of this approach, the skill or skill clusters addressed through instruction do not relate to skills needed to participate in the break or to complete the transition. In this approach, the break or transition is used as an opportunity to practice other targeted skills. For example, Ms. Roberts wants to give Damien more practice naming or identifying emotions in pictures. She asked her teaching assistant to show Damien 15 pictures of children in the classroom expressing different emotions, to model the emotion words associated with each picture, and to ask Damien to repeat the emotion word while he is waiting in line to wash his hands, get a drink of water, or transition to a different activity. These extra opportunities to practice naming or identifying emotions help build Damien's emotional literacy vocabulary but are not specifically related to supporting him to complete the transition (e.g., waiting his turn in line before getting a drink). This approach to embedded instruction is consistent with how transition-based teaching has been described by Werts, Wolery, and their colleagues in early childhood contexts (e.g., Werts et al., 1992; Wolery, Anthony, & Heckathorn, 1998) and with how embedded instruction has been described by McDonnell and colleagues. (For more examples and research involving this interpretation of embedded instruction, see Chiara, Schuster, Bell, & Wolery, 1995; Jameson, McDonnell, Johnson, Riesen, & Polychronis, 2007; Johnson & McDonnell, 2004; Johnson, McDonnell, Holzwarth, & Hunter, 2004; McDonnell, Johnson, Polychronis, & Risen, 2002; McDonnell, Johnson, Polychronis, Risen, & Kercher, 2006; Polychronis, McDonnell, Johnson, Riesen, & Jameson, 2004; Riesen, McDonnell, Johnson, Polychronis, & Jameson, 2003.)

In this chapter, we focus on an approach to embedded instruction described by Snyder and colleagues (2013) as part of a research project focused on embedded instruction for early learning (www.embeddedinstruction.net). The approach primarily aligns with the first approach described but also incorporates opportunities for massed, spaced, or distributed instructional learning trials between ongoing activities or routines or during transitions. Thus, this approach to embedded instruction would accommodate the instruction Ms. Roberts used with Sue and the instruction her assistant used with Damien. Decisions about embedding instruction, the instructional procedures to be used, and whether massed, spaced, or distributed instructional learning trials will be used depends on the type of skill being targeted and the child's phase of learning (i.e., acquisition, fluency, maintenance, generalization, adaptation; Haring et al., 1988; Wolery, Bailey, & Sugai, 1988). For social-emotional competence, this might include skills that would be categorized as dispositional (e.g., flexibility, persistence), chains of behavior (e.g., brief social interaction with a peer), discrete responses (e.g., labeling emotions represented in pictures), or response classes (e.g., social problem solving). Research on embedded instruction has generally focused on the latter three categories with little evidence related to using embedded instruction to teach dispositions (Wolery & Hemmeter, 2011).

Because social-emotional skills are often complex tasks that require either chained behaviors to engage in an interaction or contextually mediated behaviors to engage in context-specific appropriate behaviors, embedded instruction is often a logical and defensible instructional approach to support social and emotional learning. For example, to acquire, be fluent with, maintain, generalize, and adapt a skill focused on regulating the volume of speech, we would expect children to learn to vary their volume based on the context (e.g., morning circle, small group work, outside, in the lunch room) and expectations in each context and do this over time across many different situations. Thus, for meaningful use of this skill, it should be taught within and across contexts, and limited decontextualized practice would be recommended.

Defining Embedded Instruction for Early Learning and Associated Components

Embedded instruction involves providing instruction on children's priority learning goals (referred to as learning targets) during typically occurring activities, routines, and transitions. Intentional learning opportunities are embedded within and across activities, routines, and transitions rather than presented in decontextualized or nonrelevant settings. The characteristics or demands of the activity, routine, or transition; the child's motivation and preferences; and the adults, children, or materials that are part of the activity, routine, or transition set the occasion for instruction and for the child to learn social and emotional skills. The instructional strategies used during embedded instruction vary on a continuum from less structured to more structured but are intentionally planned and systematically delivered. Massed, spaced, or distributed embedded instruction learning trials are implemented depending on children's priority learning targets and their phase of learning (i.e., acquisition, fluency, maintenance, generalization, adaptation).

What to teach: Specify the instructional content. The "what to teach" component of embedded instruction involves identifying social and emotional learning content to be taught and specifying learning targets for all children, a group of children, or an individual child. For children with disabilities, an annual goal or individualized education program (IEP) goal might be used to help plan embedded instruction by breaking down the larger individualized education program goal into manageable and teachable skills that fit with preschool activities and are the focus of instruction for the child (Horn, Lieber, Li, Sandall, & Schwartz, 2000; Sandall & Schwartz, 2002, 2008). Alternatively, additional social or emotional skills not related to IEP goals might be identified to strengthen the child's social-emotional competence. To identify skills for learning targets, children or a child can be observed during activities, routines, and transitions and during interactions with adults or peers (e.g., observe how the child gains a peer's attention during free-play or on the playground). Evaluate where the child is successful and where the child may need more assistance to support his or her engagement and social-emotional learning (e.g., child looks at peers but does not greet or talk to peers). Behaviors or skills that are selected for learning targets for embedded instruction should be one or two steps ahead of what the child can currently do.

After a skill has been identified it should be written as a priority learning target to help guide the instructional plan. A learning target is a behavioral objective. It specifies the behavior or skill, the conditions under which the behavior or skill will occur, and the criteria for determining when the behavior or skill is achieved based on the child's phase of learning. Table 5.1 shows a learning target for Damien. Learning targets should be written so selected behaviors or skills are observable, age-appropriate, functional, and generative (Grisham-Brown, Hemmeter, & Pretti-Frontczak, 2005; Notari-Syverson & Shuster, 1995; Snyder et al., 2009).

Table 5.1
Learning Target Written as a Behavioral Objective

Information to include	Example
(1) The child's name.	(1) Damien will (2) greet peers by saying "hello," "hi," "what are you doing," or a similar short phrase (3) following a teacher or peer model of the same word(s) when joining peers in class activities (4) during morning arrival, centers, and in the cafeteria. (5) Damien will greet four peers following a model in at least two activities for 2 consecutive days.
(2) The behavior or what the child is expected to do or say.	
(3) The conditions or level of assistance the child requires to do the behavior.	
(4) When or where you want the child to use the behavior.	
(5) The criterion or expected performance.	

Early in the preschool year, Ms. Roberts observed Sue's and Damien's social and emotional skills during ongoing activities, routines, and transitions over the course of a week. She used her state's early learning guidelines and a social-emotional skills checklist to help structure her observations. She noticed Damien didn't join peers in play activities and avoided activities where a group of peers were gathered together (centers, morning arrival). He tended to stand back and watch from a few feet away. She suspected he wasn't sure how to approach the peers to join them in play or how to play cooperatively with them. She wrote a learning target to help Damien gain a skill that would help him approach his peers (see Table 5.1). She also wrote a learning target to help him learn cooperative play skills (e.g., take turns with a peer lining up blocks to make a road for a truck or stacking blocks to make a garage). While watching Sue, Ms. Roberts noticed that peers did not notice Sue signing "please" while looking at a toy. Ms. Roberts knew that when Sue signed "please" and looked at a toy, she expected a peer to give her the toy. However, Sue would not persist when her signs went unnoticed by her peers, and she would instead sit quietly watching. Ms. Roberts wrote a learning target for Sue related to gaining a peer's attention before signing for the item. She decided to teach Sue to tap a peer on the shoulder and then sign to ask for a toy or item from a peer. Ms. Roberts also noticed that Sue spent a lot of time alone. She didn't really have any "buddies" and would move away from peers when they got too close to her. She wrote a learning target to help Sue work or play with a buddy.

Embedded instruction focuses on systematic and intentional instruction to help children learn skills during ongoing activities, routines, and transitions. Teachers should expect to update learning targets regularly. Updates might include changing the type or level of support a child receives to do a skill (e.g., no models provided to Damien to greet peers), specifying additional activities or routines in which the child uses the skill to promote maintenance and generalization, or identifying a new skill after a child has achieved a previous skill.

When to teach: Identifying activities, routines, and transitions. Motivating and engaging activities provide opportunities to address priority learning target behaviors in logical and appropriate social contexts. By teaching in the ongoing activity, children will learn when and how to use social and emotional skills in authentic activities and social situations. This component of embedded instruction includes identifying logical and appropriate activities that are a good fit for embedded instruction and developing an activity matrix to specify when and where embedded instruction will occur. An activity matrix shows the classroom schedule and is used to plan when instruction on learning targets will occur. It has the classroom schedule listed down the left side and typically has children's names written across the top. The cells in the matrix show which learning targets will be addressed; in which activities, routines, and transitions the targets will be addressed; and how many embedded instruction trials are planned. Figure 5.1 shows an example of an activity matrix that Ms. Roberts is using for Sue's and Damien's learning targets. For example, Ms. Roberts plans to embed instruction on Sue's "tap and ask" learning target in four different activities, routines, or transitions, and the number of planned learning trials ranges from one during arrival and morning groups to five during small group.

Ms. Roberts considers several aspects of when and where to teach as she selects activities that she will use to embed instruction for Sue and Damien on their priority learning targets. First, she considers activities, routines, or transitions that are logical in relation to the learning target (e.g., when and where would Sue and Damien use or need the learning target skill?). She might also consider times she could plan environmental arrangements or peer-mediated instructional strategies to create opportunities during logical activities, routines, or transitions. Second, she considers relevant information about Sue and Damien, including current abilities, preferences, and support needs in relation to the structure, characteristics, and demands of ongoing activities, routines, and transitions. For example, although closing circle might be a logical activity in which to embed instruction on Sue's tap and ask target, Ms. Roberts' teaching assistants do not participate in closing circle, so the structure and characteristics of this activity make it difficult to provide intentional and systematic instructional learning trials on this learning target. Third, Ms. Roberts considers the number of planned embedded instruction learning opportunities to provide to Sue and Damien within and across activities, routines, and transitions for each of their learning targets in relation to instruction she and her staff are providing to other children in the classroom and the number of staff available to implement embedded instruction. Selecting activities, routines, or transitions that are a good fit for embedded learning opportunities based on the considerations described above will support implementation of embedded instruction as planned.

Ms. Roberts identified small-group activities as a possible activity to embed learning opportunities for Sue and Damien. For Sue, small group was a good fit for her learning target behavior. In many of the small group activities, Ms. Roberts limited the number of materials so children had to ask one another for items, and a teacher or teaching assistant was available during small group to prompt Sue to tap a peer on the shoulder before signing. For Damien, Ms. Roberts determined that small group was not a good fit for his learning target focused on greeting peers. After a week of implementing embedded instruction on this target during small group, Ms. Roberts decided based on the activity structure and characteristics that it was not logical for peers to greet one another when they began a small group activity led by a teacher or teaching assistant. She adjusted her activity matrix to reflect this change.

Figure 5.1
Activity Matrix for Sue and Damien

Schedule	Sue	Damien
Arrival and morning groups (8:40–9:00)	Tap/ask x 1	Greeting peers x 4
Morning circle and welcome (9:00–9:20)	Buddy activity x 1	
Free play (9:20–10:00)	Tap/ask x 2	Play skills x 2
Small group (10:00–10:20)	Tap/ask x 5	
Wash hands and snack (10:20–10:40)	Buddy activity x 1	
Center activities (10:40–11:20)	Tap/ask x 2	Play skills x 2
Outdoor play (11:20–11:50)	Buddy activity x 1	Greeting peers x 2
Potty and wash hands (11:50–12:00)		
Lunch in cafeteria (12:00–12:30)		Greeting peers x 3
Story time (12:30–12:45)	Buddy activity x 1	
Nap or quiet time (12:45–1:15)		
Music and movement or Art (1:15–1:40)	Buddy activity x 2	
Closing circle (1:40–1:50)		
Pack-up and dismissal (1:50–2:00)		

To ensure sufficient and varied learning opportunities, embedded instruction learning trials can be massed or spaced within an activity or distributed within or across activities. Decisions about whether to mass, space, or distribute learning trials are based on the child's phase of learning and the type of learning target specified. For example, embedded instruction learning trials for

Sue might be spaced across a small group activity when there are multiple opportunities to ask for toys and items as she is acquiring the "tapping before signing" skill. This would provide Sue with repeated opportunities to learn a skill that is useful based on the structure and characteristics of the activity. In contrast, embedded instruction learning trials might need to be distributed across several activities for Damien's learning target related to greeting peers. Damien is able to say the words to greet peers but needs instructional support to learn when and why to greet peers and to generalize greetings to new situations and peers.

How to teach: Using intentional and systematic instructional procedures for complete learning trials. This component of embedded instruction emphasizes use of intentional and systematic instructional procedures to teach skills and ensure sufficient opportunities to learn and respond. The type and intensity of instruction provided is informed by data related to a child's capacity for meeting environmental or learning task expectations and by examining the child's responses to the instructional procedures used and learning opportunities provided. Embedded instruction establishes contingent instructional interactions among the child, adult, and environment as well as provides a mechanism for children to acquire understanding of relationships among skills they have learned, expectations of the learning environment, and when use of skills is desirable and appropriate (McBride & Schwartz, 2003; Snyder et al., 2013). Snyder and colleagues (2013) have emphasized complete learning trials, rather than specific instructional procedures, to support a teacher's consistent use of an intentional and systematic instructional sequence. The term *complete learning trial* is used to describe the instructional sequence or interactions among teachers, children, and the environment during a teaching or learning episode. All instructional procedures use complete learning trials to promote learning. Complete learning trials include the antecedent (i.e., the prompt or naturally occurring stimulus that occasions the behavior), the behavior (i.e., learning target), and a consequence (e.g., feedback in the form of reinforcement, descriptive comment). It might be necessary to provide additional help, and this can be in the form of a prompt paired with the antecedent to support the child in a more structured interaction to ensure errorless learning. If a child does the skill with help as part of the antecedent, teachers can fade the prompt after helping a few times. Alternatively, additional help might be in the form of an error correction when the child does not do the target behavior or the attempt is incorrect. Learning occurs through complete learning trial sequences, which are particularly important for young children with learning challenges or disabilities. Table 5.2 shows how Ms. Roberts has provided a few complete learning trials for Damien.

Multiple and varied complete learning trials can be embedded across the day so that all children receive a sufficient amount of instruction to ensure learning and development of new skills. Embedded instruction requires teachers intentionally and systematically embed complete learning trials focused on identified learning targets at a sufficient rate. Embedded instruction means teachers not only focus on "teachable moments" but also ensure the frequent occurrence of planned trials and the reliable implementation of the components of these trials. These trials can be counted and measured to ensure planned instruction is occurring to support the child's learning (Bishop-Crowe, Snyder, Crow, Mullin, & Embedded Instruction for Early Learning Project, 2011).

Often, practitioners want to know how many complete learning trials are needed to support the child's learning. There is no definitive answer to this question. Additional research is needed to address questions such as how often intentional trials should be embedded, how many trials should be provided per activity or day, and the number of activities in which instruction should occur to promote child learning (Wolery & Hemmeter, 2011). Decisions regarding these questions should use an evidence-based practice framework that incorporates the individual characteristics, preferences, and needs of the child; the learning target; the child's phase of learning related to the learning target; and the values and knowledge of teachers and families about child and family preferences and motivations (Buysse & Wesley, 2006; Snyder, 2006; Winton, 2006).

Table 5.2
Complete Learning Trials for Damien

Ongoing activity (Context)	Morning arrival (Damien arrives and goes to his cubby, there is a peer standing next to him who says, "Hi Damien.")	Free play (Damien has his favorite truck on the floor and is pushing it back and forth.)
Antecedent	Ms. Roberts says, "Damien, Thomas said 'hello' to you, you say 'hello' back. Say, "Hello Thomas."	Ms. Roberts says, "That's a nice truck, let's build it a special garage to keep it safe," and she starts stacking blocks.
Behavior	Damien says "Hello Thomas."	Damien looks at Ms. Roberts for a moment and then starts stacking blocks as well.
Consequence	Thomas smiles and shows Damien his Spiderman shirt. Damien smiles.	Ms. Roberts says, "You're doing a nice job building a big garage for your truck."

How to evaluate: Instruction implemented as planned and child learning. Collecting data about both the implementation of embedded instruction and child learning is necessary to make data-based decisions to inform instructional planning. Three questions presented by Snyder and colleagues (2013) provide a framework for data-based decision making related to evaluating embedded instruction: (a) Am I doing it? (b) Is it working? and (c) Do I need to make changes?

The first question (Am I doing it?) focuses on the fidelity with which embedded instruction learning trials are implemented. To examine the instruction implemented, consider collecting data on (a) the number of embedded instruction learning trials provided on a learning target within and across activities, and (b) whether the learning trials implemented were complete learning trials (i.e., included the antecedent, behavior, and consequence). Use this type of fidelity information to determine if instruction is being implemented as planned or whether teachers need additional implementation supports.

The second question (Is it working?) focuses on monitoring child progress and learning in relation to the learning target behavior. Collect data on child progress during ongoing activities, routines, and transitions in the classroom, not in special "testing" situations. The type of child progress data collected will be guided by the criterion specified in the learning target. If the criterion focuses on using a skill more often or in new settings, teachers might record tallies of how often and when a child uses the skill. If the criterion focuses on how well the child uses the skill, teachers might record data on how much help is needed to do the skill. Use the information collected to determine if the child has reached the criterion set in the learning target.

The third question (Do I need to make changes?) focuses on examining both fidelity data and child progress data to determine if changes are needed. Based on the information collected, changes might be needed in relation to the implementation of embedded instruction, the learning target(s) to be addressed, or both. Data might also suggest that the embedded instruction plan is working and that the child is making progress but has not yet achieved the desired criterion; in these cases, the instructional plan might continue without changes.

Ms. Roberts has been helping Damien greet at least five peers per day every day, and it seems to be working. She has noticed that he is looking at and saying "hi" to his peers more and more without help. She plans to count how many peers he greets when he arrives in the morning 2 days in a row without help. Both days he greeted five peers. Satisfied with his progress, Ms. Roberts decides to revise her learning target for Damien to include a back-and-forth exchange between Damien and a peer. Unfortunately, Sue is not making as much progress. Ms. Roberts asks her assistant to count to see how many times they are creating opportunities and providing a model for Sue to tap a peer to get his or her attention during the day. The assistant reports that the team created six opportunities during the day but only provided a model one time. Ms. Roberts realizes that Sue is not making progress because they are not following their instructional plan. Sue likely needs the model to learn the skill. She posts a large activity matrix on the teachers' bulletin board with a note about providing a model to help remind her and the team to implement their instructional plan.

Putting It All Together

Embedded instruction is an intentional and systematic approach that promotes child engagement, participation, and learning within everyday activities, routines, and transitions. By using an embedded instruction approach, teachers, other team members, and families have tools to address skills related to strengthening social-emotional competence by using practices focused on what to teach, when to teach, how to teach, and how to evaluate. Table 5.3 provides a tip sheet for each component of embedded instruction presented by Snyder and colleagues (2013). With this approach to embedded instruction, complex social skills that are often chained together in successive sequences of complete learning trials (i.e., a repetition of antecedent, behavior, consequence) during social interactions can be broken into manageable and teachable skills with teachers using intentional instructional opportunities to support child learning. With the right support, children can learn key social and emotional skills necessary to navigate their social environments, express their emotions in appropriate ways, and make and maintain lasting friendships.

Table 5.3
Tips for Teachers

Component	Tips for teachers
What to teach	• Target skills that are one or two steps ahead of what the child can currently do (zone of proximal development). • Start with two or three learning targets and update them as needed. • Write it down! Writing it down helps you and the team be more intentional about teaching the learning target. • Share the learning targets with the child's family to help promote learning at home and school.
When to teach	• Use peers to provide supports and model key skills. Say, "Look at what Kieran is doing, try to do it too." • Provide multiple opportunities to practice skills; repeated practice leads to mastery. • Incorporate children's interests into your ongoing activities. For example, if a child really enjoys trains, you might use a toy train during your small group game to show whose turn it is; for example, say, "When the train stops at your station it's your turn." • Review your daily schedule; plan logical opportunities to work on the skills during ongoing activities. • Use an activity matrix to write down your plan. (See the example activity matrix for Damien and Sue.)
How to teach	• It's as simple as A-B-C (antecedent-behavior-consequence). • Plan how you might create an opportunity and provide encouragement. • Provide help early so the child knows what to do, but remember to fade help so the child can learn to do the skill independently. • Use peers to help create opportunities or provide encouragement. • If the child does not do the skill, show him or her what to do for next time.
How to evaluate	• Decide on what and when to collect data (know what you are counting). • Write it down! Trying to remember what happened during the day is too hard; keep a notebook, use post-it notes, or make a data collection form and put it on a clipboard. • Ask your team to help with data collection. • Use a video camera to record your implementation of embedded instruction and watch the video to make sure all your learning opportunities have an A, B, and C.

Note. Adapted with permission from "Using Embedded Instruction to Support Young Children's Learning," by T. McLaughlin, P. Snyder, & M. L. Hemmeter, *Exchange Magazine*, September/October 2011, pp. 53–56.

References

Bishop-Crowe, C., Snyder, P., Crow, R., Mullin, M., & Embedded Instruction for Early Learning Project. (2011). *Embedded instruction for early learning observation system—Teacher version (EIOS-T).* [Manual and training videos]. Unpublished instrument. College of Education, University of Florida, Gainesville, FL.

Bricker, D., & Cripe, J. (1992). *An activity-based approach to early intervention.* Baltimore, MD: Brookes.

Buysse, V., & Wesley, P. W. (2006). Making sense of evidence-based practice: Reflections and recommendations. In V. Buysse & P. W. Wesley (Eds.), *Evidence-based practice in the early childhood field* (pp. 227–246). Washington, DC: Zero to Three.

Chiara, L., Schuster, J. W., Bell, J. K., & Wolery, M. (1995). Small-group massed-trial and individually-distributed-trial instruction with preschoolers. *Journal of Early Intervention, 19,* 203–217. http://dx.doi.org/10.1177/105381519501900305

Connors-Tadros, L. (2013). Research and information on social and emotional learning to inform birth through age five standards revision. *CEELO FASTfacts,* New Brunswick, NJ: Center on Enhancing Early Learning Outcomes. Available at www.ceelo.org

Denham, S. A. (2006). Social-emotional competence as a support for school readiness: What is it and how do we assess it? *Early Education and Development, 17,* 57–89. http://dx.doi.org/10.1207/s15566935eed1701_4

Dodge, K. (2011, March). Introduction: Why focus on social-emotional learning? In K. Dodge, S. Jones, & P. Tolan (Eds.), *New findings on approaches to improving children's social and emotional learning: Implications for academic performance and behavior.* Briefing held at the biannual meeting of the Society for Research in Child Development, Montreal, Canada. Available at http://casel.org/publications/powerpoints-from-hhs-presentation/

Domitrovich, C. E., Cortes, R. C., & Greenberg, M. T. (2007). Improving young children's social and emotional competence: A randomized trial of the preschool PATHS curriculum. *The Journal of Primary Prevention, 28,* 67–91. http://dx.doi.org/10.1007/s10935-007-0081-0

Fantuzzo, J. W., Bulotsky-Shearer, R., Fusco, R. A., & McWayne, C. (2005). An investigation of preschool classroom behavioral adjustment problems and social-emotional school readiness. *Early Childhood Research Quarterly, 20,* 259–275. http://dx.doi.org/10.1016/j.ecresq.2005.07.001

Fox, L., & Hanline, M. F. (1993). A preliminary evaluation of learning within developmentally appropriate early childhood settings. *Topics in Early Childhood and Special Education, 13,* 308–327. http://dx.doi.org/10.1177/027112149301300308

Grisham-Brown, J., Hemmeter, M. L., & Pretti-Frontczak, K. L. (2005). *Blended practices for teaching preschoolers in inclusive settings.* Baltimore, MD: Brookes.

Grisham-Brown, J., Pretti-Frontczak, K., Hawkins, S. R., & Winchell, B. N. (2009). Addressing early learning standards for all children within blended preschool classrooms. *Topics in Early Childhood Special Education, 29,* 131–142. http://dx.doi.org/10.1177/0271121409333796

Grisham-Brown, J., Schuster, J. W., Hemmeter, M. L., & Collins, B. C. (2000). Using an embedding strategy to teach preschoolers with significant disabilities. *Journal of Behavioral Education, 10*, 139–162.

Haring, N. (1988). *Generalizations for students with severe handicaps: Strategies and solutions.* Seattle, WA: University of Washington Press.

Hart, B. M., & Risley, T. R. (1974). Using preschool materials to modify the language of disadvantaged children. *Journal of Applied Behavior Analysis, 7*, 243–256. http://dx.doi.org/10.1901/jaba.1974.7-243

Hart, B. M., & Risley, T. R. (1975). Incidental teaching of language in the preschool. *Journal of Applied Behavior Analysis, 8*, 411–420. http://dx.doi.org/10.1901/jaba.1975.8-411

Horn, E., & Banerjee, R. (2009). Understanding curriculum modifications and embedded learning opportunities in the context of supporting all children's success. *Language, Speech, and Hearing Services in Schools, 40*, 406–415. http://dx.doi.org/10.1044/0161-1461(2009/08-0026)

Horn, E., Lieber, J., Li, S., Sandall, S., & Schwartz, I. (2000). Supporting young children's IEP goals in inclusive settings through embedded learning opportunities. *Topics in Early Childhood and Special Education, 20*, 208–223. http://dx.doi.org/10.1177/027112140002000402

Horner, R. (2005). General case programming. In M. Hersen, J. Rosqvist, A. Gross, R. Drabman, G. Sugai, & R. Horner (Eds.), *Encyclopedia of behavior modification and cognitive behavior therapy* (Vol. 3, pp. 1343–1348). Thousand Oaks, CA: SAGE.

Jameson, J. M., McDonnell, J., Johnson, J., Riesen, T., & Polychronis, S. (2007). A comparison of one-to-one embedded instruction in the general education classroom and one-to-one massed practice instruction in the special education classroom. *Education and Treatment of Children, 30*, 23–44. http://dx.doi.org/10.1353/etc.2007.0001

Johnson, J. W., & McDonnell, J. (2004). An exploratory study of the implementation of embedded instruction by general educators with students with developmental disabilities. *Education and Treatment of Children, 27*, 46–63.

Johnson, J. W., McDonnell, J., Holzwarth, V. N., & Hunter, K. (2004). The efficacy of embedded instruction for students with developmental disabilities enrolled in general education classes. *Journal of Positive Behavior Interventions, 6*, 214–227. http://dx.doi.org/10.1177/10983007040060040301

Losardo, A., & Bricker, D. (1994). Activity-based intervention and direct instruction: A comparison study. *American Journal of Mental Retardation, 98*, 744–765.

Malmskog, S., & McDonnell, A. P. (1999). Teacher-mediated facilitation of engagement by children with developmental delays in inclusive preschools. *Topics in Early Childhood Special Education, 19*, 203-216. http://dx.doi.org/10.1177/027112149901900401

McBride, B. J., & Schwartz, I. S. (2003). Effects of teaching early interventionists to use discrete trials during ongoing classroom activities. *Topics in Early Childhood and Special Education, 23*, 5–17. http://dx.doi.org/10.1177/027112140302300102

McDonnell, J., Johnson, J., & McQuivey, C. (2008). Embedded instruction for students with developmental disabilities in general education classrooms. *DDD Prism Series* (Vol. 6). Arlington, VA: Council for Exceptional Children.

McDonnell, J., Johnson, J., Polychronis, S., & Risen, T. (2002). Effects of embedded instruction on students with moderate disabilities enrolled in general education classes. *Education and Training in Mental Retardation and Developmental Disabilities, 37*, 363–377.

McDonnell, J., Johnson, J., Polychronis, S., Risen, T., & Kercher, K. (2006). Comparison of one-to-one embedded instruction in general education classes with small group instruction in special education classes. *Education and Training in Developmental Disabilities, 41*, 125–138.

McLaughlin, T., Snyder, P., & Hemmeter, M. L. (2011). Using embedded instruction to support young children's learning. *Exchange Magazine, September/October Edition*, 53–56.

National Education Goals Panel. (1996). *The National Education Goals report: Building a nation of learners.* Washington, DC: U.S. Government Printing Office.

Notari-Syverson, A. R., & Shuster, S. L. (1995). Putting real life skills into IEPs/IFSPs for infants and young children. *TEACHING Exceptional Children, 27*, 29–32.

Odom, S., McConnell, S., & Brown, W. (2008). Social competence of young children: Conceptualization, assessment, and influences. In W. Brown, S. Odom, & S. McConnell (Eds.), *Social competence of young children: Risk disability and intervention* (pp. 117–140). Baltimore, MD: Brookes.

Polychronis, S. C., McDonnell, J., Johnson, J. W., Riesen, T., & Jameson, M. (2004). A comparison of two trial distribution schedules in embedded instruction. *Focus on Autism and Other Developmental Disabilities, 19*, 140–151. http://dx.doi.org/10.1177/10883576040190030201

Pretti-Frontczak, K., & Bricker, D. D. (2001). Use of the embedding strategy by early childhood education and early childhood special education teachers. *Infant and Toddler Interventions: The Transdisciplinary Journal, 11*, 111–128.

Riesen, T., McDonnell, J., Johnson, J. W., Polychronis, S., & Jameson, M. (2003). A comparison of constant time delay and simultaneous prompting within embedded instruction in general education classes with students with moderate to severe disabilities. *Journal of Behavioral Education, 12*, 241–259.

Rule, S., Losardo, A., Dinnebeil, L. A., Kaiser, A., & Rowland, C. (1998). Research challenges in naturalistic intervention. *Journal of Early Intervention, 21*, 283–293.

Sandall, S. R., & Schwartz, I. S. (2002). *Building blocks for teaching preschoolers with special needs.* Baltimore, MD: Brookes.

Sandall, S. R., & Schwartz, I. S. (2008). *Building blocks for teaching preschoolers with special needs* (2nd ed.). Baltimore, MD: Brookes.

Schepis, M. M., Reid, D. H., Ownbey, J., & Parsons, M. B. (2001). Training support staff to embed teaching within natural routines of young children with disabilities in an inclusive preschool. *Journal of Applied Behavior Analysis, 34*, 313–327. http://dx.doi.org/10.1901/jaba.2001.34-313

Snell, M. (2007). Advances in instruction. In S. L. Odom, R. H. Horner, M. E. Snell, & J. Blacher, J. (Eds.), *Handbook of developmental disabilities* (pp. 249–268). New York, NY: Guilford.

Snyder, P. (2006). Best available research evidence: Impact on research in early childhood. In V. Buysse & P. W. Wesley (Eds.), *Evidence-based practice in the early childhood field* (pp. 35–70). Washington, DC: Zero to Three.

Snyder, P., Hemmeter, M. L., McLaughlin, T., Algina, J., Sandall, S., & McLean, M. (2011, April). *Impact of professional development on preschool teachers' use of embedded-instruction practices.* Paper presented for the American Educational Research Association annual conference, New Orleans, LA.

Snyder, P., Hemmeter, M. L., Sandall, S., McLean, M., & McLaughlin, T. (2013). Embedded instruction practices in the context of response to intervention. In V. Buysse & E. Peisner-Feinberg (Eds.), *Handbook of response-to-intervention in early childhood* (pp. 283–298). Baltimore, MD: Brookes.

Snyder, P., McLaughlin, T., Sandall, S., McLean, M., Hemmeter, M. L., Crow, R., … Embedded Instruction for Early Learning Project. (2009). *LTRS: Learning target rating scale.* [Manual]. Unpublished instrument. College of Education, University of Florida, Gainesville, FL.

Snyder, P., Rakap, S., Hemmeter, M. L., McLaughlin, T., Sandall, S., & McLean, M. (2014). Naturalistic instructional approaches in early learning: A systematic review of the empirical literature. *Journal of Early Intervention.* Manuscript accepted for publication.

Vaughn, S., Kim, A. H., Morris Sloan, C. V., Hughes, M. T., Elbaum, B., & Sridhar, D. (2003). Social skills interventions for young children with disabilities: A synthesis of group design studies. *Remedial and Special Education, 24,* 2–15. http://dx.doi.org/10.1177/074193250302400101

Venn, M. L., Wolery, M., Werts, M. G., Morris, A., DeCesare, L. D., & Cuffs, M. S. (1993). Embedding instruction in art activities to teach preschoolers with disabilities to imitate their peers. *Early Childhood Research Quarterly, 8,* 277–294. http://dx.doi.org/10.1016/s0885-2006(05)80068-7

Werts, M. G., Wolery, M., Holcombe-Ligon, A., Vassilaros, M. A., & Billings, S. S. (1992). Efficacy of transition based teaching with instructive feedback. *Education and Treatment of Children, 15,* 320–334.

Winton, P. J. (2006). The evidence-based practice movement and its effect on knowledge utilization. In V. Buysse & P. W. Wesley (Eds.), *Evidence-based practice in the early childhood field* (pp. 71–115). Washington, DC: Zero to Three.

Wolery, M., Anthony, L., & Heckathorn, J. (1998). Transition-based teaching: Effects on transitions, teachers' behavior, and children's learning. *Journal of Early Intervention, 21,* 117-131. http://dx.doi.org/10.1177/105381519802100205

Wolery, M., Bailey, D., & Sugai, G. (1988). *Effective teaching: Principles and procedures of applied behavior analysis with exceptional students.* Needham, MA: Allyn and Bacon.

Wolery, M., & Hemmeter, M. L. (2011). Classroom instruction: Background, assumptions, and challenges. *Journal of Early Intervention, 33,* 371–380. http://dx.doi.org/10.1177/1053815111429119

Chapter 6

Maximizing Social Competence Through Family and Caregiver Interventions

L. Lynn Stansberry-Brusnahan, Terri Vandercook, and Kelly J. Whalon

Meaningful relationships were identified as one of five valued life outcomes that families indicated as critical to achieving a high quality of life for their children (Giangreco, Cloninger, Mueller, Yuan, & Ashworth, 1991). That meaningful relationships are important to both adults and their children should come as no surprise. Friendships in particular are a special type of relationship. "Friendship is about choice and chemistry and cannot even be readily defined, much less forced. This is precisely its magic" (Van der Klift & Kunc, 2002, p. 23).

The overwhelmed parents of a young child, Collin, expressed to his educator that the social challenges resulting from their son's disability undermined their confidence in their caregiving abilities and generated doubts about being able to meet Collin's needs. One of the hardest things for these parents to come to terms with was that their son might never have friends. The school professionals knew that Collin spent most of his waking hours at home under his parents' care and that as professionals they transition in and out of his life. Thus, these educators recognized the need to support Collin's parents in their desire for him to make friends.

Collin's educators recognize the benefits of partnering with families. Caregivers are instrumental to their child's social development, and their influence begins from the earliest parent-child interactions (Guralnick, 2010; Sheridan, Knoche, & Marvin, 2008). Similar to teachers, caregivers deem friendships are important (Hollingsworth & Buysse, 2009), which make them helpful partners in addressing social goals. Partnering with families may even be essential to the social development of children with autism spectrum disorder (ASD) or other developmental disabilities (DD) because caregivers arrange many of the social opportunities that can lead to friendships and greater peer networks (Freeman & Kasari, 2002; Guralnick, 2010). In addition, children with ASD or other DD need multiple opportunities to interact socially (McCollum & Ostrosky, 2008), and by partnering with families it is possible to create a comprehensive plan that targets the social goals of children with ASD or other DD in a variety of contexts (Sheridan et al., 2008).

Nevertheless, there are a number of factors that influence the extent to which caregivers create social opportunities for their children with disabilities (see Sheridan et al., 2008 for a review), including available supports and resources, stress level, and cultural expectations for social development (Guralnick, 2010; McCollum & Ostrosky, 2008; Sheridan et al., 2008). For example, levels of caregiver stress and available supports impact the extent to which caregivers feel they can influence their child's development (Trivette et al., 2010). Therefore, it is imperative that one of the goals of forming partnerships is to enhance caregiver feelings of self-efficacy, or their belief that when they intervene at home they can make a difference in the social development of their child (McCollum & Ostrosky, 2008). A capacity-building model has led to increases in caregiver feelings of competence (Trivette, Dunst, & Hamby, 2010). This model involves professionals sharing information, identifying existing family strengths and resources, and supporting caregivers in their use and mastery of effective strategies and practices (see Swanson, Raab, & Dunst, 2011; Woods & Brown, 2011). As caregivers implement these strategies and begin to see a difference in their child's learning and development, caregivers' feelings of efficacy improve, which in turn encourages continued strategy use, enhances caregiver feelings of empowerment, and ultimately results in positive outcomes for the child (see Trivette, Dunst, & Hamby, 2010). In fact, research suggests that when caregivers are empowered to intervene at home there is greater generalization of skills, reduced levels of caregiver stress, and increased family leisure time (Ingersoll & Wainer, 2012).

When building relationships with caregivers, it is also important that (a) caregivers are seen as true partners, (b) their cultural beliefs and values are understood and respected, and (c) their role in decision making is encouraged and valued (Woods & Brown, 2011). In a collaborative partnership, the views of caregivers and professionals are shared with the common goal of developing a cohesive educational plan designed to improve child outcomes (Sheridan et al., 2008). To be implemented effectively, the strategies caregivers employ must meet their needs while specifically addressing their child's social goals (Geisthardt, Brotherson, & Cook, 2002). Effective partnerships with families emphasize the following components: (a) addressing social skills and communication in natural environments, (b) supporting and enhancing caregiver-child interactions, (c) shared decision making, and (d) use of evidence-based practices shown to enhance social competence (Sheridan et al., 2008).

This chapter will emphasize each of these components of effective partnerships to improve the social interaction of children with ASD or other DD. Although most of the research on partnering with families stems from the early intervention literature, emerging research suggests that similar models should be applied with families of school-age children (Ingersoll & Wainer, 2012). More specifically, in this chapter we provide (a) examples of evidence-based, naturalistic strategies that can enhance parent-child interactions that are influential to social development, (b) opportunities and strategies designed to support children with ASD or other DD when interacting with peers at home, (c) suggestions for expanding peer networks using natural supports, and (d) ideas for providing caregiver training sessions at school.

Using Naturalistic Teaching Strategies at Home

Educators can support caregiver implementation of naturalistic teaching strategies at home. Naturalistic interventions are provided in natural environments or places where children and youth spend their time, which more effectively promotes development (Jung, 2007; Raab &

Dunst, 2004). Naturalistic strategies are designed to encourage specific skills that are naturally reinforcing (Franzone, 2009; Pindiprolu, 2012). Because these strategies are most advantageous when embedded in naturally occurring routines, caregivers make logical intervention agents as they establish a number of natural routines throughout the child's day.

Research supports the effectiveness of caregiver-implemented interventions (Hendricks, 2009; Odom, Collet-Klingenberg, Rogers, & Hatton, 2010). A caregiver-implemented intervention entails caregivers directly using evidence-based strategies to increase the number of learning opportunities and the acquisition of important skills (Hendricks, 2009; Koegel, Symon, & Koegel, 2002). For example, caregivers have successfully served as intervention agents in studies addressing the social, behavioral, and communication development of children with ASD (Odom et al., 2010). Studies have reported that caregivers' use of naturalistic teaching strategies has a positive impact on a number of developmental skills (Hancock & Kaiser, 2002; Kaiser & Roberts, 2013; Koegel et al., 2002; Nunes & Hanline, 2007; Woods, Kashinath, & Goldstein, 2004), including social communication (McConachie & Diggle, 2006). Moreover, caregivers not only learn but also generalize and maintain their use of naturalistic teaching strategies (Kaiser & Roberts, 2013; Tekin-Iftar, 2008).

Pindiprolu (2012) conducted a literature review to analyze the components of effective naturalistic interventions, such as incidental teaching (Hart & Risley, 1975; McGee, Almeida, Sulzer-Azaroff, & Feldman, 1992), pivotal response training (Koegel et al., 2002; Pierce & Schreibman, 1997), and naturalistic language teaching paradigm (Kaiser, Yoder, & Keetz, 1992; Laski, Charlop, & Schreibman, 1988). Common to all of these interventions was a focus on child interests and use of natural consequences. In general, naturalistic interventions included the following four steps: (a) arrange the environment, (b) follow the child's lead, (c) elicit the target skills, and (d) provide natural reinforcement (see Franzone, 2009; Pindiprolu, 2012).

Step 1. Arrange Environment and Set Up Opportunities

Six strategies can be used to arrange the environment to elicit communication and social interaction during typically occurring routines at home or in the community. These strategies create many opportunities to address a variety of communication functions in everyday activities. If these strategies are embedded in a variety of typical routines and with multiple communication partners, the maintenance and generalization of these skills are enhanced (Schlosser & Lee, 2000; Stokes & Baer, 1977). The six strategies are:

1. **Requesting access to preferred items:** Place preferred objects out of reach, thus setting up the opportunity for the child to request the preferred objects.

2. **Asking for help:** Utilize objects that require assistance, thus setting up the opportunity for the child to ask for help.

3. **Asking for more:** Provide only a few of a preferred object or engage the child in an activity for only a short time, thus setting up an opportunity for the child to ask for more.

4. **Greeting:** Arrange for a new person to enter or exit the home, a room, or an activity, thus setting up the opportunity for the child to verbalize greetings, farewells, requests for someone to join an activity in progress, or responses to the requests to join the activity.

5. **Refusing:** Give the child something he or she does not like, thus setting up the opportunity for the child to refuse.

6. **Choice making:** Provide a choice of food or activity, thus setting up the opportunity for the child to make a choice.

Step 2. Follow Child's Lead

Naturalistic interventions are often initiated when the child expresses an interest in materials or activities (Ingersoll, 2010). That is, the adult carefully engineers the environment to include preferences and interests that capture the attention of and motivate children and youth to interact with others. This may involve the caregiver providing initial wait time by looking expectantly at the child in order to encourage an initiation. For example, the child may look, reach, name, request, or gesture toward an item in a carefully arranged environment. It is important to wait for the child to initiate, which can include more subtle behaviors, such as eye gaze. Waiting for the child to initiate provides an opportunity to shape communication to more clearly reflect the child's intent, thus increasing the likelihood the message will be understood by multiple communication partners.

Step 3. Elicit Target Skills

When using naturalistic strategies, the caregiver's first task is to set up the environment (Step 1) to elicit an initiation from the child (Step 2). Then, the caregiver patiently waits for the child to initiate or respond to the environmental arrangement. Both verbal approximation and nonverbal behaviors are immediately interpreted as an initiation, and the caregiver models a more advanced initiation for the child to imitate (Step 3).

Step 4. Provide Natural Reinforcement

Immediately following a correct or scaffolded initiation or response, the caregiver provides contingent, natural reinforcement (i.e., access to the preferred item or activity, avoidance of the item or activity refused, and/or help or assistance). Natural reinforcement is considered a natural consequence of the communication attempt made by the child. Access to the item happens for a particular amount of time as the caregiver engages the child further during the activity to extend the interaction.

Caregiver-Implemented Examples

The four steps outlined above occur in a natural sequence. For example, a caregiver places her child's favorite book on a shelf out of his reach. The child responds by pointing to the book or looking at the book. As the child points or looks at the book, the caregiver says, "It looks like you want the book. Say, 'book please.'" Immediately after the child imitates the caregiver's model, he receives access to the book (i.e., natural reinforcement). The caregiver extends the interaction by reading the book with the child.

If a student is unable to initiate verbally and uses an augmentative communication device, then the use of naturalistic teaching strategies mirrors that outlined previously but incorporates the use of the device. For example, during snack time the caregiver says, "Do you want fruit snacks or a granola bar today?" as she holds each item in front of the child. The child reaches for fruit snacks without accessing his communication device. The caregiver says, "It looks like you want the fruit snacks. Tell me, 'fruit snacks please.'" She points to the symbols of the fruit snacks and the word "please" on the communication device. If the child does not respond, the caregiver provides as little physical support as necessary for the child to activate the "fruit snacks" and "please" icons on the communication device. Immediately after requesting the item, the child is given the fruit snacks. The caregiver expands the conversation (while gesturing to the communication device) by saying, "My favorite color of fruit snack is orange, what is yours?"

Supporting Caregivers in Their Implementation of Naturalistic Teaching Strategies

There are a number of ways educators can share naturalistic teaching strategies with families. For instance, educators may choose to model the strategies outlined previously at school or on a home visit. In addition, weekly letters to families can include strategies that address a social goal. For example, one of Collin's social goals is to ask for help. Collin's teacher sent a note home to Collin's mother explaining ways she can set up opportunities for Collin to ask for help at home. Collin's teacher incorporated in her suggestions information she gathered from Collin's mother earlier in the school year regarding family routines and Collin's preferences. Table 6.1 provides multiple examples of all four steps outlined in this section. These examples can be readily shared with caregivers and are easily tailored to the interests and preferences of children and youth with ASD or other DD.

Facilitating Play Dates at Home

Mrs. Martinez is Collin's second-grade teacher at Friendship School. Collin is included in the general education classroom with support from the special education teacher, Ms. Shannon. Collin's mother expressed to both Mrs. Martinez and Ms. Shannon that she is concerned that Collin has yet to make friends at school. Collin's older sister was invited over to the houses of her classmates and neighbors for play dates and birthday parties since she started school, but Collin has yet to receive an invitation. Mrs. Martinez and Ms. Shannon are providing opportunities for Collin to interact with his peers at school, but both teachers agree that there would be greater continuity and opportunity for Collin to make progress toward his social competence goals if he had opportunities to socially interact with peers outside of school.

Table 6.1
Opportunities for Communication and Social Interaction

Arrange environment	Follow child's lead	Elicit target skill	Provide natural reinforcements	Material examples
Place preferred objects or items out of reach.	Child points or looks toward object.	Interpret child's behavior as communicative. Provide a communication model for the child to imitate verbally or use the child's communication device.	Provide access to the preferred item that was out of reach and engage in further interaction with the item if possible.	Books on a shelf, games, snacks or toys in a cupboard, snacks in a refrigerator, remote control on a shelf, objects representing outdoor activities (e.g., bike helmet, bucket of sidewalk chalk, basketball).
Utilize objects that require assistance.	Child hands object to caregiver or points to objects with expectant or frustrated look.	Interpret child's behavior as a request for help. "You want help?" Provide a communication model for the child to imitate verbally or use the child's communication device.	Provide assistance so that the child can use the object alone or with someone if they are interested.	Container of a preferred beverage (e.g., juice box, milk carton), food item (e.g., peanut butter jar, pickle jar) or activity (e.g., bubbles, bucket of chalk, toy box).

Table 6.1 (continued)
Opportunities for Communication and Social Interaction

Arrange environment	Follow child's lead	Elicit target skill	Provide natural reinforcements	Material examples
Provide only a small amount of a preferred object or engage in a preferred activity for only a short time period.	Child points to or holds up an empty bowl or points to a blank video screen.	Interpret child's behavior as wanting more. "You want more _____?" Provide a communication model for the child to imitate verbally or use the child's communication device.	Provide more of the object or activity time.	Snacks, magnetic letters, colored markers, pencils, crayons, paint, Play-Doh, LEGO®, cars, dolls, sidewalk chalk, utensils to blow bubbles, bubble solution, and so on.
Arrange for a new person to enter or exit home, room, or activity.	Child looks at person entering or exiting.	Interpret child's behavior as noticing the person. "You saw Jill come in." Provide a communication model for the child to imitate verbally or use the child's communication device.	Person provides a return greeting or farewell and interacts in some way (e.g., joins activity, chats for a minute).	Knock at front door or doorbell rings, person enters room and greets child, person moves toward activity in progress.

Table 6.1 *(continued)*
Opportunities for Communication and Social Interaction

Arrange environment	Follow child's lead	Elicit target skill	Provide natural reinforcements	Material examples
Give child nonpreferred object or ask if child wants to engage in a nonpreferred activity.	Child shakes head no, pushes away, or moves away.	Interpret as not interested. "You don't want ____?" Provide a communication model for the child to imitate either verbally or use the child's communication device.	Allow the child to avoid the undesired item or activity.	Food, activities, clothing, and so on.
Provide choices of something the child needs or wants.	Child verbalizes, looks, or points at preferred object or activity.	Expand upon or confirm child's choice. "You chose ____, here you go," or "You chose ____." Provide a communication model for the child to imitate either verbally or use the child's communication device.	Provide opportunity to receive and use or engage in the object or activity alone or with someone else who is interested.	Food, board games, card games, video games, television shows, movies, DVDs, CDs, bike routes, clothing, and so on.

Children regularly participate in play dates throughout childhood (Werner, Vismara, Koegel, & Koegel, 2006), and these opportunities to interact with peers lead to the development of social competence (Ladd & Hart, 1992) and lasting friendships (Frankel, Gorospe, Chang, & Sugar, 2011). Research suggests that children are more comfortable engaging with peers, demonstrate greater social behavior, and are more socially accepted when they interact with peers outside of school

(Sheridan et al., 2008). Therefore, increasing the frequency and improving the quality of play dates may help support the development of friendships between children with ASD or other DD and their peers (Frankel et al., 2011; Hollingsworth & Buysse, 2009). In a recent observational study, the number of play dates children with ASD participated in was positively correlated with two findings: (a) higher rates of reciprocal peer interactions on the playground, and (b) peer reception of social initiations (Frankel et al., 2011). Yet children with disabilities spend little time interacting with peers at home (Geisthardt et al., 2002). Because families are instrumental in the process of arranging play dates and encouraging the relationships of their children (Freeman & Kasari, 2002; Guralnick, Neville, Connor, & Hammond, 2003), educators can support families to create opportunities for developing friendships outside of school (Geisthardt et al., 2002; McCollum & Ostrosky, 2008).

Although the research on establishing play dates has been primarily conducted in schools (Jull & Mirenda, 2011), emerging research shows that play dates at home can facilitate gains in skills that promote social competence. For example, play dates between children with ASD and their siblings or peers at home have led to increased social interactions and/or engagement in reciprocal play (Baker, 2000; Jull & Mirenda, 2011; Koegel, Werner, Vismara, & Koegel, 2005; Maione & Mirenda, 2006; Strain & Danko, 1995). Two studies included the use of contextual supports to facilitate a successful play date: (a) incorporating activities that are reinforcing for both the child with ASD and his or her peers, and (b) ensuring the activity includes a cooperative arrangement so that both children have an essential, interactive role in completing the activity (Jull & Mirenda, 2011; Koegel, et al., 2005). Researchers have embedded cooperative arrangements in a number of activities (e.g., baking, dress-up, bike riding, crafts, science experiments, games). For example, a caregiver may create roles in a baking activity with one peer measuring and the other pouring ingredients. This cooperative arrangement is designed so that the active roles children are assigned require interaction to complete the activity (see Koegel et al., 2005).

Adult facilitation is important for a successful play date (Jull & Mirenda, 2011; Werner et al., 2006). For example, educators are excellent resources to assist families in identifying peers who show interest in interacting with their children or who share a preferred interest (Werner et al., 2006). In addition, caregivers can use a variety of strategies to encourage interaction during a play date (Jull & Mirenda, 2011; Werner et al., 2006). Jull and Mirenda (2011) taught parents to (a) prepare the activity in advance to include prepping materials and instructing children on their roles in the activity, (b) limit materials so that children have to share (e.g., only one measuring cup), (c) stay in proximity of children without sitting or standing directly next to them (e.g., sitting or standing behind children), (d) minimize distracting stimuli, and (e) provide prompts and contingent praise (Jull & Mirenda, 2011). Prompts were primarily delivered to the play date (Jull & Mirenda, 2011), but prompts can also be provided to the child with ASD or other DD. Prompts may be used to facilitate requesting (e.g., items, materials, help; "Ask your friend, 'can I have the red paint?'"), initiating comments (e.g., "Tell your friend, 'your picture looks great!'"), offering materials (e.g., "Tell your friend, 'your turn.'"), securing attention ("Say, 'look!'"), or initiating a new activity (e.g., "Ask your friend, 'what do you want to do next?'"). These prompting types encourage an interaction during the play date and increase the number of opportunities children have to learn from social interaction (Strain & Danko, 1995; Werner et al., 2006). Educators can provide caregivers with sample scripts of each type of prompt to use during a play date to encourage an interaction. It is important that adults fade support as children begin engaging with one another spontaneously (Werner et al., 2006).

Mrs. Martinez has developed a list of peers who show an interest in spending time with Collin and who share his interest in insects. Mrs. Martinez and Ms. Shannon decide to talk with Collin's mother about the possibility of setting up a play date at home. After Collin's mother expressed an interest in facilitating a play date, Mrs. Martinez contacted the caregivers of Collin's peers to determine their interest. Those interested provided contact information for Mrs. Martinez to share with Collin's mother. Mrs. Martinez shared activities from an insect unit she taught in the past and brainstormed some other activity ideas with Collin's mother. Collin's mother thought Collin would be most interested in a baking, craft, and outdoor activity. Mrs. Martinez and Ms. Shannon created a handout for Collin's mother that included instructions for making dirt cake with worms, creating spider webs, and going on a bug hunt. In their handout, Mrs. Martinez and Ms. Shannon included scripts of prompts to facilitate an interaction between Collin and his peers that focused on his social competence goals of initiating comments and sharing. They also included scripted prompts so that Collin would be able to secure the attention of his peer and request items. This would make the completion of the activity contingent on Collin interacting with his peer. Mrs. Martinez and Ms. Shannon reviewed the handout and prompts with Collin's mother. Table 6.2 includes information from the handout, including selected insect activities with directions, possible roles, web sites with additional instructions and demonstrations, and sample prompts to encourage an interaction.

Because children with ASD may not be intrinsically motivated to socially engage with peers, incorporating interests is important (Jull & Mirenda, 2011; Koegel et al., 2005). Involving children in preparation also can increase motivation (Werner et al., 2006). For example, Collin and his mother took pictures of insects in their backyard to make the insect checklist for their bug hunt activity, and Collin helped his mother shop for the ingredients to make the dirt cake. For some children, priming may also help prepare the child for the play date (Werner et al., 2006). Priming gives the child with ASD or other DD an opportunity to become familiar with the activity prior to the play date, which can increase the child's comfort level and make the task more predictable. For example, Mrs. Martinez and Ms. Shannon included a YouTube video in their handout of a young child making dirt cake with worms. The video includes a step-by-step demonstration and scripted comments. Collin's mother showed the video to Collin before his play date arrived.

Collin's mother was so happy with Collin's first play date that she began to come up with new activities. Mrs. Martinez and Ms. Shannon have noticed a change in Collin. His peers are initiating toward Collin more on the playground, and Collin received his first invitation to a birthday party from one of his play date peers. Mrs. Martinez and Ms. Shannon have decided to work with other teachers at Friendship Elementary School to host a play date night where they plan to teach all interested families how to facilitate play dates between children with ASD or other DD and their peers. They were excited to learn that not only families of children with ASD or other DD signed up, but so did the families of some general education students who would like to include children with ASD or other DD in their future play dates.

Table 6.2
Play Date Activities and Prompts

Activity	Possible roles	Steps for preparation	Prompts to promote interaction
Making "dirt cake with worms"	Measurer, pourer, whisker, Oreo smasher, gummy-worm keeper	Handout of directions to make "dirt cake": • Needed materials (e.g., instant chocolate pudding mix, Cool Whip, Oreo cookies, gummy worms, clear plastic cups) • Recipe directions handwritten, printed from a web site, or web site link provided or • Search for a YouTube video demonstration of making dirt cake to show at home or school prior to the play date	Prompt to secure attention: • "Say, 'Look!' And show your friend your cup of dirt." Prompt to share: • "What color gummy worms do you want?" • "It's your turn to whisk the milk." Prompt to request: • "Can I smash the Oreos now?" Prompt to comment: • "You are fun to cook with." • "This cake looks gross." • "Want to go on a bug hunt when we finish?"

Table 6.2 *(continued)*
Play Date Activities and Prompts

Activity	Possible roles	Steps for preparation	Prompts to promote interaction
Spider webs with friends	Yarn cutter, keeper of the plastic spiders/ scissors/glue/ insects	Handout of directions for making spider webs: • Materials needed (e.g., paper plates, scissors, different colors of yarn that will be visible on the paper plate color, glue, plastic spiders and other plastic insects) • Written directions for making the spider webs (e.g., Cut slits around the plate. Tape the yarn to the back of the plate and wrap around the plate through the slits. Glue spiders on the web), printed directions from a web site, or web site addresses with directions	Prompt to secure attention: • "Look!" Prompt to share: • "What color yarn do you want?" • "Do you want a spider for your web?" Prompt to request: • "Can I use the glue?" • "Where should I put the spider?" Prompt to comment: • "That spider is cool!" • "Your web is great!" Prompt to initiate a new activity: • "Let's go eat our dirt cake!"

Table 6.2 *(continued)*
Play Date Activities and Prompts

Activity	Possible roles	Steps for preparation	Prompts to promote interaction
Bug scavenger hunt	Bug checklist completer, photographer, keeper of the magnifying glass/net/clear container with air holes keeper	Handout of directions for a bug scavenger hunt: • Materials needed (e.g., clear container with air holes; net; magnifying glass; picture or checklist of bugs from your backyard; camera) • Directions for creating a written or visual checklist of harmless bugs children can find in your backyard (e.g., ladybug, beetle, ant, caterpillar, worm, grasshopper, butterfly) • Directions regarding how to use the materials to find bugs, capture bugs, or take a picture of the bugs found. Directions can be printed from a web site source (e.g., http://www.scholastic.com/parents/resources/article/science-nature-activities/bug-hunt) or a list of web sites can be provided (if the family has internet access)	Prompt to secure attention: • "Look!" or "Over here!" Prompt to share: • Do you want to use the magnifying glass?" • "It is your turn to use the net." Prompt to request: • "Can I use the magnifying glass?" • "Where should we look first?" Prompt to comment: • "That bug is cool!" • "Good job spotting that ladybug!" Prompt to initiate a new activity: • "What do you want to play next?"

Communicating with families about progress is also important. Letting families know of any social progress at school and asking families about their child's social progress at home can help instructional planning. Collin's teachers, Mrs. Martinez and Ms. Shannon, created a quick and easy-to-complete journal page for Collin's mother (See Figure 6.1). This sheet keeps Mrs. Martinez and Ms. Shannon informed about Collin's progress toward his social goals at home and also encourages active, ongoing communication with Collin's mother.

Figure 6.1
Take-Home Progress Monitoring Form

Date of play date:	
How was Collin's play date?	
How often did Collin initiate comments?	Not at all 1 2 3 4 5 Frequently
How often were Collin's initiations prompted?	Not at all 1 2 3 4 5 Frequently
How often did Collin spontaneously offer to share?	Not at all 1 2 3 4 5 Frequently

Utilizing Natural Supports

Educators can support the development of social relationships that can become friendships by providing caregivers with ideas on how to capitalize on natural family and community supports to enhance their child's quality of life and provide opportunities to practice social skills, make friends, and promote generalization. Communities and family life are full of opportunities for children and youth to develop supportive relationships with peers, explore strengths and interests, learn important social skills, and make valuable connections, such as friendships. Too often, however, participation by children and youth with ASD or other DD is restricted to "special" programs that depend wholly on the presence of paid support and adults. Professionals can encourage families to think beyond special services and paid supports as the only opportunities for the development of skills. Existing family life and community programs can readily be drawn upon to more naturally support the development of friendships. Natural environments provide opportunities to practice targeted skills in multiple, naturally occurring contexts and thereby promote generalization.

In this chapter, we define *natural supports* as personal associations and relationships developed in the home and community that enhance the quality of life for children and youth with DD. These natural supports include, but are not limited to, the family and home, the neighborhood and the broader community, and associations developed through participation in clubs, organizations, and other civic activities. Natural supports can enhance the social integration of individuals with ASD or other DD and are more permanent and more readily available than paid supports. A structure for planning for natural supports is the Systematic Plan for Achieving Natural Supports (Trach & Mayhall, 1997), which includes an ecological assessment (See Introduction and Chapter 1) to (a) determine individual needs and available or potential natural supports, (b) match natural supports to identified needs, and (c) develop plans to utilize supports to build social competence. The following list includes potential natural supports: family; friends; neighborhoods; clubs and social organizations; civic, professional, and nonprofit organizations; recreation centers; volunteer opportunities; education opportunities; child care; online communities; religious and faith communities; sports and hobbies; schools and students; co-workers and job sites.

Providing Structured Caregiver Training

Educators can support the development of social relationships that can become friendships by setting up structured caregiver training. Caregivers may need to be taught how to provide naturalistic interventions to elicit target social skills and how to utilize peer and natural supports (Franzone, 2009). Caregivers can be taught how to implement interventions through structured training programs. It is important to remember that intervention goals for the individual child or youth will guide caregiver training. The following recommendations are important considerations when creating caregiver training (Hendricks, 2009; Ingersoll & Wainer, 2012).

Choosing Instructional Training Format and Location

Create an efficient and cost-effective format to provide training to caregivers (Koegel et al., 2002). Consider caregiver preferences, and provide training to individual caregivers, groups of caregivers, or a combination of both individuals and groups (Brookman-Frazee, Stahmer, Baker-Ericzén, & Tsai, 2006). Some parents may require one-to-one problem-solving and intensive instruction, whereas other caregivers and components may be taught in groups. Remember that providing group opportunities allows caregivers to learn from interacting with other caregivers (Sofronoff, Leslie, & Brown, 2004). It would be typical and constructive to utilize a combination of approaches. Consider geographical constraints when designing training. Decide if you will provide training at a caregiver's home, in a community setting, or at a school.

Choosing Training Components

Design training taking into consideration adult learning, ability to retain knowledge, application, and generalization skills. For example, it is important when teaching adults that there are multiple opportunities for learners to absorb, apply, process or reflect, and self-assess their own learning (Trivette, Dunst, Hamby, & O'Herin, 2010). Facilitators must also consider the intensity and detail of instruction and provide opportunities for caregivers to practice strategies in relevant ways (Koegel, Koegel, Harrower, & Carter, 1999). Table 6.3 provides examples of different training modes that can be effectively used in combination.

Table 6.3
Training Modality Definitions

Training modality	Defined
Direct instruction	Lecture or discussion format that includes detailed descriptions of strategies. Discuss concerns and allow questions.
Model and demonstration	Strategies to allow caregivers to observe both good and poor implementation examples.
Role-play and rehearsal	Strategies that allow caregivers time to practice intervention prior to implementation with child or youth.
Video demonstrations	Watch videotapes of strategies to see examples and steps of intervention.
Coaching with feedback	Coach caregivers to implement interventions with child or youth. Emphasize correctly implemented skills and provide immediate corrective strategies to improve caregiver's implementation skills.
Analysis and feedback	With the caregiver, watch a video of the caregiver engaged with the child or youth. Allow questions, discuss concerns, and review progress.
Performance feedback	Collect data and document implementation and duration of targeted strategies with the child or youth. Note successes, challenges, and/or concerns.

Choosing Training Amount and Duration

Decide on the amount and duration of training based on the characteristics and needs of the child and caregivers, then monitor progress. The goal is to teach caregivers to implement intervention strategies consistently over time, across settings, and with a variety of skills without direct support from the educator. Over time, caregivers should become more independent and master targeted skills and strategies.

Encouraging Participation

It can be difficult for families to attend school trainings, and it can take additional resources. Ingersoll and Wainer (2012) provided a number of suggestions to encourage attendance, including providing childcare, offering transportation or training in an easily accessible location, flexible scheduling (trainings held after work hours), providing food, and offering rewards or incentives. Partnering with local agencies and/or universities can also be helpful. Many college students may volunteer childcare, some organizations may have locations within walking distance for some families, and so on. If possible, educators should make occasional home visits to support caregiver implementation of the recommended practices.

Final Thoughts

As school professionals, we know that the students we work with will spend more time under their caregivers' watch than ours, and that these students will eventually age out of the educational system. Our professional goals should include training and supporting caregivers to implement instructional programs for their children and youth with ASD or other DD. Educators should expose caregivers to peer support strategies and natural supports that can be implemented in their homes, neighborhoods, and communities. When educators partner with caregivers, fears can subside as children experience greater socialization. The friendships Collin has established were created through an effective caregiver-teacher partnership, and the resulting relationships have been truly magical.

With the help of Collin's educators, every year the list of Collin's natural supports and friends grew. For example, in high school Collin's parents and physical education teacher worked together to encourage him to participate in cross country. Being part of a team provided Collin with a natural opportunity to interact with peers. Collin joined and gained the respect and acceptance of the team because he did his best to stay with them during runs and never quit when he was tired. Being on the team gave Collin a social function to attend every Friday night as the group got together for pasta dinners and set goals. One of the team leaders approached the coach and said he was inspired by Collin, who had simple goals like keeping his shoelaces from coming undone and to not accidentally stray off the course. After high school, his teammates headed off for different colleges across the country, but they remained connected to Collin through social media and visited him when they were home for school breaks. By working with educational professionals and providing opportunities for natural supports, Collin enjoys a rich social life filled with friends. His parents state Collin has an enviable social calendar and more friends than they do.

References

Baker, M. J. (2000). Incorporating the thematic ritualistic behaviors of children with autism into games: Increasing social play interactions with siblings. *Journal of Positive Behavior Interventions, 2*, 66–84. http://dx.doi.org/10.1177/109830070000200201

Brookman-Frazee, L., Stahmer, A., Baker-Ericzén, M., & Tsai, K. (2006). Parenting interventions for children with autism spectrum and disruptive behavior disorders: Opportunities for cross-fertilization. *Clinical Child and Family Psychology Review, 10,* 181–200. http://dx.doi.org/10.1007/s10567-006-0010-4

Frankel, F. D., Gorospe, C. M., Chang, Y., & Sugar, C. A. (2011). Mothers' reports of play dates and observation of school playground behavior of children having high-functioning autism spectrum disorders. *Journal of Child Psychology and Psychiatry, 52,* 571–579. http://dx.doi.org/10.1111/j.1469-7610.2010.02318.x

Franzone, E. (2009). *Naturalistic intervention: Steps for implementation.* Madison, WI: University of Wisconsin National Professional Development Center on Autism Spectrum Disorders and Waisman Center.

Freeman, S. F. N., & Kasari, C. (2002). Characteristics and qualities of the play dates of children with Down syndrome: Emerging or true friendships? *American Journal on Mental Retardation, 107,* 16–31. http://dx.doi.org/10.1352/0895-8017(2002)107<0016:caqotp>2.0.co;2

Geisthardt, C. L., Brotherson, M. J., & Cook, C. C. (2002). Friendships of children with disabilities in the home environment. *Education and Training in Mental Retardation and Developmental Disabilities, 37,* 235–252.

Giangreco, M., Cloninger, C., Mueller, P., Yuan, S., & Ashworth, S. (1991). Perspectives of parents whose children have dual sensory impairments. *The Journal of the Association for Persons with Severe Handicaps, 16,* 14–24.

Guralnick, M. J. (2010). Early intervention approaches to enhance the peer-related social competence of young children with developmental delays: A historical perspective. *Infants & Young Children, 23*(2), 73–83. http://dx.doi.org/10.1097/iyc.0b013e3181d22e14

Guralnick, M. J., Neville, B., Connor, R. T., & Hammond, M. A. (2003). Family factors associated with the peer social competence of young children with mild delays. *American Journal on Mental Retardation, 4,* 272–287. http://dx.doi.org/10.1352/0895-8017(2003)108<272:ffawtp>2.0.co;2

Hancock, T. B., & Kaiser, A. P. (2002). The effects of trainer-implemented enhanced milieu teaching on the social communication of children with autism. *Topics in Early Childhood Special Education, 22,* 39–54. http://dx.doi.org/10.1177/027112140202200104

Hart, B. M., & Risley, T. R. (1975). Incidental teaching of language in the preschool. *Journal of Applied Behavior Analysis, 8,* 411–420. http://dx.doi.org/10.1901/jaba.1975.8-411

Hendricks, D. R. (2009). *Parent-implemented intervention for children with autism spectrum disorders: Online training module.* Chapel Hill, NC: University of North Carolina National Professional Development Center on Autism Spectrum Disorders and FPG Child Development Institute.

Hollingsworth, H. L., & Buysse, V. (2009). Establishing friendships in early childhood inclusive settings: What roles do parents and teachers play? *Journal of Early Intervention, 31,* 287–307. http://dx.doi.org/10.177/1053815109352659

Ingersoll, B. R. (2010). Teaching social communication: A comparison of naturalistic behavioral and development, social pragmatic approaches for children with autism spectrum disorders. *Journal of Positive Behavior Interventions, 12*, 33–43. http://dx.doi.org/10.1177/1098300709334797

Ingersoll, B., & Wainer, A. (2012). Incorporating parent training into school curricula for children with autism spectrum disorders (pp. 207–225). In P. Mundy & A. M. Mastergeorge (Eds.), *Educational interventions for students with autism.* San Francisco, CA: Wiley.

Jull, S., & Mirenda, P. (2011). Parents as play date facilitators for preschoolers with autism. *Journal of Positive Behavior Interventions, 13*, 17–30. http://dx.doi.org/10.1177/1098300709358111

Jung, L. A. (2007). Writing individualized family service plan strategies that fit into the ROUTINE. *Young Exceptional Children, 10*(3), 21–27.

Kaiser, A. P., & Roberts, M. Y. (2013). Parent-implemented enhanced milieu teaching with preschool children with intellectual disabilities. *Journal of Speech, Language, and Hearing Research, 56*(1), 295–309. http://dx.doi.org/10.1044/1092-4388(2012/11-0231)

Kaiser, A. P., Yoder, P. J., & Keetz, A. (1992). Evaluating milieu teaching. In S. F. Warren & J. Reichle (Eds.), *Causes and effects in communication and language intervention* (pp. 9–47). Baltimore, MD: Brookes.

Koegel, L. K., Koegel, R. L., Harrower, J. K., & Carter, C. M. (1999). Pivotal response intervention I: Overview of approach. *Journal of the Association for Persons with Severe Handicaps, 24*, 174–185. http://dx.doi.org/10.2511/rpsd.24.3.174

Koegel, R. L., Symon, J. B., & Koegel, L. K. (2002). Parent education for families of children with autism living in geographically distant areas. *Journal of Positive Behavior Interventions, 4*, 88–103. http://dx.doi.org/10.1177/109830070200400204

Koegel, R. L., Werner, G. A., Vismara, L. A., & Koegel, L. K. (2005). The effectiveness of contextually supported play date interactions between children with autism and typically developing peers. *Research and Practice for Persons with Severe Disabilities, 30*, 93–102. http://dx.doi.org/10.2511/rpsd.30.2.93

Ladd, G. W., & Hart, C. H. (1992). Creating informal play opportunities: Are parents' and preschoolers' initiations related to children's competence with peers? *Developmental Psychology, 28*, 1179–1187. http://dx.doi.org/10.1037//0012-1649.28.6.1179

Laski, K. E., Charlop, M. H., & Schreibman, L. (1988). Training parents to use the natural language paradigm to increase their autistic children's speech. *Journal of Applied Behavior Analysis, 21*, 391–400. http://dx.doi.org/10.1901/jaba.1988.21-391

Maione, L., & Mirenda, P. (2006). Effects of video modeling and video feedback on peer-directed social language skills of a child with autism. *Journal of Positive Behavior Interventions, 8*, 106–118. http://dx.doi.org/10.1177/10983007060080020201

McCollum, J. A., & Ostrosky, M. M. (2008). Family roles in young children's emerging peer-related social competence. In W. H. Brown, S. L. Odom, & S. R. McConnell (Eds.), *Social competence of young children: Risk, disability, & intervention* (pp. 31–61). Baltimore, MD: Brookes.

McConachie, H., & Diggle, T. (2006). Parent implemented early intervention for young children with autism spectrum disorder: A systematic review. *Journal of Evaluation in Clinical Practice, 13*(1), 120–129. http://dx.doi.org/10.1111/j.1365-2753.2006.00674.x

McGee, G. G., Almeida, M., Sulzer-Azaroff, B., & Feldman, R. S. (1992). Promoting reciprocal interactions via peer incidental teaching. *Journal of Applied Behavior Analysis, 25*(1), 117–126. http://dx.doi.org/10.1901/jaba.1992.25-117

Nunes, D., & Hanline, M. F. (2007). Enhancing the alternative and augmentative communication use of a child with autism through a parent-implemented naturalistic intervention. *International Journal of Disability, Development and Education, 54*(2), 177–197. http://dx.doi.org/10.1080/10349120701330495

Odom, S. L., Collet-Klingenberg, L., Rogers, S. J., & Hatton, D. D. (2010). Evidence-based practices in interventions for children and youth with autism spectrum disorders. *Preventing School Failure, 54*, 275–282. http://dx.doi.org/10.1080/10459881003785506

Pierce, K., & Schreibman, L. (1997). Multiple peer use of pivotal response training to increase social behavior of classmates with autism: Results from trained and untrained peers. *Journal of Applied Behavior Analysis, 30*, 157–167. http://dx.doi.org/10.1901/jaba.1997.30-157

Pindiprolu, S. S. (2012). A review of naturalistic interventions with young children with autism. *Journal of the International Association of Special Education, 13*(1), 69–78.

Raab, M., & Dunst, C. J. (2004). Early intervention practitioner approaches to natural environment interventions. *Journal of Early Intervention, 27*, 15–26. http://dx.doi.org/10.1177/105381510402700102

Schlosser, R. W., & Lee, D. (2000). Promoting generalization and maintenance in augmentative and alternative communication: A meta-analysis of 20 years of effectiveness research. *Augmentative and Alternative Communication, 16*, 208–227. http://dx.doi.org/10.1080/07434610012331279074

Sheridan, S. M., Knoche, L. L., & Marvin, C. A. (2008). Competent families, competent children: Family-based interventions to promote social competence in young children. In W. H. Brown, S. L. Odom, & S. R. McConnell (Eds.), *Social competence of young children: Risk, disability, & intervention* (pp. 301–320). Baltimore, MD: Brookes.

Sofronoff, K., Leslie, A., & Brown, W. (2004). Parent management training and Asperger syndrome: A randomized controlled trial to evaluate a parent based intervention. *Autism, 8*, 301–317. http://dx.doi.org/10.1177/1362361304045215

Stokes, T. F., & Baer, D. M. (1977). An implicit technology of generalization. *Journal of Applied Behavior Analysis, 10*, 349–367. http://dx.doi.org/10.1901/jaba.1977.10-349

Strain, P. S., & Danko, C. D. (1995). Caregivers' encouragement of positive interaction between preschoolers with autism and their siblings. *Journal of Emotional and Behavioral Disorders, 3*, 2–12. http://dx.doi.org/10.1177/106342669500300101

Swanson, J., Raab, M., & Dunst, C. J. (2011). Strengthening family capacity to provide young children everyday natural learning opportunities. *Journal of Early Childhood Research, 9*, 66–80. http://dx.doi.org/10.1177/147676718X10368588

Tekin-Iftar, E. (2008). Parent-delivered community-based instruction with simultaneous prompting for teaching community skills to children with developmental disabilities. *Education and Training in Developmental Disabilities, 43*, 249–265.

Trach, J. S., & Mayhall, C. D. (1997). Analysis of the types of natural supports utilized during job placement and development. *Journal of Rehabilitation, 63*(2), 43–48.

Trivette, C. M., Dunst, C. J., & Hamby, D. W. (2010). Influences of family-systems intervention practices on parent-child interactions and child development. *Topics in Early Childhood Special Education, 30*, 3–19. http://dx.doi.org/10.1177/0271121410364250.

Trivette, C. M., Dunst, C. J., Hamby, D. W., & O'Herin, C. E. (2010). Effects of different types of adaptations on the behavior of young children with disabilities. *Research Brief (Tots n Tech Research Institute), 4*(1), 1–26. Retrieved from http://tnt.asu.edu/files/Adaptaqtions_Brief_final.pdf

Van der Klift, E., & Kunc, N. (2002). Beyond benevolence: Supporting genuine friendships in inclusive schools. In J. S. Thousand, R. A. Villa, & A. I. Nevin (Eds.), *Creativity and collaborative learning: The practical guide to empowering students, teachers, and families* (2nd ed., pp. 21–28). Baltimore, MD: Brookes.

Werner, G. A., Vismara, L. A., Koegel, R. L., & Koegel, L. K. (2006). Play dates, social interactions, and friendships. In R. L. Koegel & L. K. Koegel (Eds.), *Pivotal response treatments for autism: Communication, social and academic development* (pp. 199–216). Baltimore, MD: Brookes.

Woods, J., & Brown, J. A. (2011). Integrating family capacity-building and child outcomes to support social communication development in young children with autism spectrum disorder. *Topics in Language Disorder, 31*, 235–246. http://dx.doi.org/10.1097/tld.0b013e318227fde4

Woods, J., Kashinath, S., & Goldstein, H. (2004). Effects of embedding caregiver-implemented teaching strategies in daily routines on children's communication outcomes. *Journal of Early Intervention, 26*, 175–193. http://dx.doi.org/10.1177/105381510402600302

Chapter 7

Developing Effective Peer Networks
Erik W. Carter, Heartley B. Huber, and Matthew E. Brock

Devin would make a great friend. He has a quirky sense of humor, a knack for pulling clever pranks, a love of country music, and a passion for sports. But few other students at Columbia High School even know Devin, let alone are aware of his many strengths. Like most other students with severe disabilities at his school, Devin spends relatively little time in the same classes or clubs as his peers without disabilities. Although his teachers and parents want to involve him more fully in the life of the school, they wonder how best to support such participation.

During the fall semester, Devin attended two general education classes: American history and computer science. The special education teacher assigned a new paraprofessional, Ms. DeStazio, to support Devin in both classes. Initially worried about disrupting other students, Ms. DeStazio chose to sit with Devin near the back of the classroom. This also made it possible for them to arrive a few minutes after the bell rang and leave a few minutes early to more easily navigate the often-crowded hallways. Ms. DeStazio was focused on ensuring Devin completed his daily assignments in class, and she worked individually with him even as other students in the class worked in small groups. She hoped other students in the class might reach out to get to know Devin, but they rarely did. By the end of the semester, Devin had learned quite a bit about American history and how to navigate a computer. But he rarely had talked with anyone other than Ms. DeStazio, and he had no friends.

Ms. DeStazio sensed her constant presence might be a barrier to interactions with other students and to Devin's involvement in some class activities, but she wasn't sure what alternatives might exist. Moreover, she was somewhat reluctant to fade back her direct support because she might be viewed by the classroom teacher as "not doing her job." Besides, if she didn't help Devin, who else would?

For students similar to Devin, schools typically present a combination of potential opportunities and clear challenges. Although inclusive education has been advocated for a host of philosophical, legal, and empirical reasons (Jackson, Ryndak, & Wehmeyer, 2008/2009), most schools still struggle to involve students with severe disabilities (e.g., autism spectrum disorder, intellectual disability, multiple disabilities) in the breadth of learning and relationship opportunities that make up everyday school life. This chapter addresses peer support arrangements as an evidence-based approach for supporting students with extensive support needs to participate academically and socially in middle and high school activities.

Fostering Relationships and Learning in Inclusive Settings

Over the last few decades, students with severe disabilities in the United States have spent increasingly more of their school day outside of special education classrooms (McLeskey, Landers, Williamson, & Hoppey, 2012). One rationale for this gradual shift in educational placement has been the diverse learning opportunities that exist within the general education curriculum (Browder & Spooner, 2011; Jackson et al., 2008/2009). But it is the rich social opportunities existing within inclusive settings that perhaps have garnered the most attention in conversations about why inclusion matters. When designed well, participation in general education classrooms can provide students with increased opportunities to learn and practice important social and communication skills, view models of appropriate social behavior among their peers, and meet peers with shared interests. As students work alongside and get to know their peers without disabilities, students with disabilities may develop new friendships and expanded peer networks that enhance their sense of belonging and improve overall quality of life (Carter, Bottema-Beutel, & Brock, 2014; Katz & Mirenda, 2002).

These potential academic and social benefits do not accrue simply because students are enrolled in general education classrooms. Indeed, descriptive studies confirm students can be just as socially isolated in a general education classroom as in a special education classroom (e.g., Carter, Sisco, Brown, Brickham, & Al-Khabbaz, 2008; Chung, Carter, & Sisco, 2012). Where students with severe disabilities spend their school day certainly matters, but how students are supported to participate in those settings may matter even more.

Considering Alternatives to Individually Assigned Adult Support

As emphasis on increasing access to the general education curriculum has intensified, so have questions about how best to support the involvement of students with severe disabilities in inclusive classrooms. Increasingly, schools are turning to one-to-one paraprofessional support models as a primary avenue for promoting general education participation (Giangreco, Suter, & Doyle, 2010). However, this heavy reliance on individually assigned adult supports may introduce a host of unintended consequences, particularly in middle and high schools. For example, research suggests the constant presence of a paraprofessional can hinder interactions with peers, foster dependence on adults, increase challenging behaviors, limit interactions with general education teachers, and set students apart (e.g., Carter & Kennedy, 2006; Giangreco, Doyle, & Suter, 2012). Advocates also have raised concerns about the appropriateness of assigning the least trained staff in a school to assist students with the most extensive support needs (Giangreco & Broer, 2007). The absence of empirical support for individually assigned adult support within inclusive classrooms has led researchers to suggest a number of alternatives to this widespread educational approach.

Peer Support Arrangements as an Evidence-Based Practice

Peer support arrangements offer an evidence-based alternative to an exclusive reliance on paraprofessional support in inclusive classrooms. Peer support models involve teaching one or more peers without disabilities in the same general education class to provide targeted academic, social, and behavioral supports to their classmate with severe disabilities (Carter, Cushing, & Kennedy, 2009). After participating in an initial orientation, students work together throughout the semester while accessing needed support and facilitation from the paraprofessional. As these students gain experience and increased confidence, the paraprofessional looks for opportunities to fade direct support and shift to a broader role within the classroom. Although primarily advocated as a new role for paraprofessionals, other school staff (e.g., special educators, general educators, related services providers) can also serve as facilitators of peer support arrangements.

What might the impact of these support models be on participating students and staff? For students with severe disabilities, research suggests peer support arrangements may be associated with increases in social interactions, communication skills, access to support, academic engagement, and friendships (see Carter & Kennedy, 2006; Carter, Sisco, Chung, & Stanton-Chapman, 2010). Research suggests peers without disabilities may benefit academically from their involvement, develop new perspectives on disability and inclusion, and gain valued relationships (Copeland et al., 2004; Cushing & Kennedy, 1997). For educators, this intervention is considered feasible to implement within everyday middle and high school classrooms (Carter & Pesko, 2008). Last, paraprofessionals report they appreciate having more explicit guidance on their roles within inclusive classrooms and interacting with a broader range of students (Carter, Moss, Hoffman, Chung, & Sisco, 2011).

Implementing Peer Support Arrangements in Inclusive Classrooms

Peer support arrangements represent one of many approaches to delivering peer-mediated interventions in inclusive schools. Although they should be adapted to meet the needs of specific students in particular classrooms, peer support arrangements typically involve the following steps: (a) preparing and planning for peer supports, (b) recruiting peers, (c) orienting students to their roles, (d) supporting students as they work together, (e) reflecting on the impact, and (f) extending interactions beyond the classroom.

Preparing and Planning for Peer Supports

Before launching a new peer support arrangement, it is important for the facilitator to develop a strong plan that addresses (a) how students will work with and support one another during various class activities, and (b) how the social and learning needs of the focal student (i.e., student with severe disabilities) will be met. A strong peer support plan should be individualized, consider the strengths and needs of the focal student, and align well with the particular classroom context. We recommend general and special educators reflect together on the following questions:

- What are the standards informing curricula, instruction, and assessment in this class?

- What expectations does the general education teacher hold for all students in this class?

- What individualized education program goals will the student work on in this class?
- Which supports will the student need to progress on these standards, expectations, and goals?
- Who will provide each of these supports?

Although several planning tools can be drawn upon to support inclusion (e.g., Cushing, Clark, Carter, & Kennedy, 2005; Jorgensen, McSheehan, & Sonnenmeier, 2010), it is especially helpful to clearly delineate the roles of peers and paraprofessionals in providing support and to detail what participation will look like for the student with severe disabilities (see Figure 7.1). This involves having the planning team reflect on typical activities and routines within the class, determining how the student with severe disabilities will participate in each, and deciding on the types of support he or she will need. For example, the team might consider whether the student could participate independently, with assistive technology or adaptive equipment, or with occasional or ongoing support from peers or adults. The team might then generate a peer support plan outlining how peers and adults will be involved in providing some or all of the needed supports. For example, during lab experiments in a biology class, the student would listen to teacher directions, help gather materials for the experiment, and work with peers to carry out the experiment. Peers would share their materials with the student, offer opportunities for the student to make choices about and provide input into the experiment, converse about the assignment, and encourage the student to use his or her communication device. The paraprofessional would facilitate social interactions, provide positive feedback to students, and offer suggestions for how the peers might work together. All of these ideas would be recorded on a planning sheet that is referenced when initially training and subsequently supporting students (see Figure 7.1).

Recruiting Peers

Among the most important steps when establishing peer support arrangements is to identify interested peers who will be effective in these roles. The classroom teacher, special educator, and/or paraprofessional should work collaboratively to consider which students might be most appropriate to invite. Although research has not yet addressed the most important qualifications for serving as a peer support, some characteristics are worth considering. Although teams may be inclined to focus only on high-achieving students, peers who are themselves struggling academically often make excellent peer supports and may even benefit academically from their involvement (Cushing & Kennedy, 1997). Based on our own work with schools, we recommend identifying students who have consistent attendance, demonstrate willingness to help other students, model positive behaviors, have good interpersonal skills, and seem eager to learn new skills. In addition, consider involving students who either have an existing relationship with or have demonstrated some interest in getting to know the student with a disability.

Multiple avenues exist for picking specific students. When students with severe disabilities are able to communicate their preferences, facilitators should ask students who they enjoy talking with, who they would like to get to know, and/or who they already consider to be a friend. The classroom teacher will likely have insight into which peers already get along well with the student or would benefit personally from assuming this role within the classroom. Last, observing in the classroom can provide helpful information about which peers work well together in groups or already interact with the student. Although finding interested peers is usually not difficult, it is important to remember that the choice of peers is likely to impact whether friendships ultimately develop and extend beyond the classroom.

Figure 7.1
Example Peer Support Plan

Class:	U.S. History	Student:	Devin
Teacher:	Ms. DeStazio	Peers:	Stephan and Mason

Typical activities and routines	Expectations for all students	Needed adaptations and supports	Roles of peers in providing support
Whole-class instruction.	When Ms. DeStazio lectures, students should listen, take notes, and respond to questions; students should contribute at least once in all group discussions.	Devin needs guided notes on which he records key words.	Devin will check his notes against those of his peers and ask questions as needed.
Small-group instruction.	Students read historical vignettes and prepare group responses based on available information; students also work in groups to prepare for occasional debates on historical topics.	When working in groups, Devin benefits from occasional redirection and extra assistance with using the technology to access information.	Peers prompt Devin to share his ideas or answer a question using his communication device; they also help him research relevant information on the Internet.
Independent work.	Students complete reflection questions and short readings to prepare for discussions and exams.	Devin needs readings copied to his tablet to use his document reader.	After finishing their work, peers will discuss selected reflection questions and record Devin's responses.
Homework and assignments.	Students complete daily assigned readings and weekly vocabulary tests.	Devin completes abbreviated quizzes with multiple choice responses; some readings are substituted.	Peers help Devin review content in advance of his quiz and talk through incorrect answers.
Needed materials.	Reading packet, textbook, notebook.	All readings are available electronically.	Peers help Devin access readings on his tablet.
Other expectations.	All students should be respectful, work well with others, and keep a detailed planner.	Devin uses a planner application on his tablet instead of a physical planner.	Peers help Devin program his assignments into his planner and make introductions to classmates.

After potential peers have been identified, the facilitator and/or classroom teacher can individually approach students before or after class to invite their involvement. In some cases, broad invitations can be extended to anyone in the class who might be interested. In either case, the facilitator should emphasize the general goal of the peer support arrangement (e.g., to help the student with a disability participate more fully in the class), describe what is involved in providing this support (e.g., sitting next to the student, helping the student participate in various class activities, talking with one another during appropriate times).

Orienting Students to Their Roles

Orientation meetings are designed to provide students with the initial information and connections they need to get started within a peer support arrangement. These meetings can be held in a quiet place at lunch, before or after school, in a study hall, or during class (when appropriate), and meetings typically take less than one hour. The adult facilitator describes why peer support strategies benefit students and are a desirable alternative to relying entirely on adult support. The facilitator then shares background information about the focal student, including his or her strengths, interests, behavior, and typical interaction style. Next, the facilitator highlights the primary goals of the peer support arrangement for the focal student (e.g., to promote interactions with peers, to teach communication skills, to increase involvement in class activities). The facilitator emphasizes the importance of peers using respectful language and respecting one another's privacy. For example, it is perfectly acceptable to share information about the student's strengths or interests in a social situation, but it is not okay to discuss a student's challenging behaviors with others. In addition, the facilitator shares general expectations related to their involvement (e.g., sitting next to the student, assisting during particular class activities, making introductions to other classmates, encouraging communication device use) along with specific strategies drawn directly from the peer support plan. Last, the facilitator emphasizes that peers will have ongoing support and can ask for additional assistance anytime they need it. The students then share any questions they have about their involvement. An outline of potential orientation meeting topics is displayed in Table 7.1 (Carter et al., 2009; Carter et al., 2011).

Table 7.1
Topics to Address During Orientation Sessions With Participating Students

- The importance of involving students in working with and supporting one another
- General information about one another's strengths, interests, and communication preferences
- General learning and social goals for the classroom
- The importance of not sharing personal or confidential information
- Expectations for the classroom or other settings in which students will work together
- Basic strategies for providing support and/or teaching new skills
- Strategies for using technology or communication devices
- Ideas for how best to motivate and encourage one another using constructive feedback
- Avenues for promoting participation in ongoing activities
- Ways to encourage social interaction with others in the classroom when appropriate
- When to ask for help from educators, paraprofessionals, and other school staff
- Any additional roles and responsibilities specific to the classroom

Supporting Students as They Work Together

Before students begin working together in the classroom, the paraprofessional and classroom teacher should talk through a number of logistical issues, such as when seating arrangements will change, how materials will be shared, and the new roles of the paraprofessional. Because many students with severe disabilities are accustomed to always having an adult by their side, it is important to let the student with a disability know about upcoming changes in support and to orient the student to any new expectations before starting the peer support arrangement.

During the first week or two of the peer support arrangement, the paraprofessional will continue to provide some support to the focal student as peers gain experience and confidence working together. During this time, the paraprofessional can use a number of facilitation strategies to promote interactions and shared learning, such as modeling ways to interact, identifying things students have in common, helping peers interpret unusual or challenging behaviors, redirecting interactions away from adults and back to one another, and ensuring students remain in proximity to one another and involved in shared activities (Feldman & Matos, 2013). By initially remaining fairly close by, the paraprofessional can readily model effective support strategies, facilitate shared activities, and ensure students are interacting appropriately. For example, if a student needs materials for a class assignment, the paraprofessional might prompt the peer to either remind or assist the student. Checking in with the students regularly to find out what is going well and where additional support is needed is critical.

Initially, peers usually benefit from ongoing monitoring and consistent feedback. Over time, however, the goal is to increase the student's independence by fading adult support. For some peer support arrangements, this fading can occur fairly quickly; for others, it will take more time. Gradually, the paraprofessional should step back, observe students as they work together, and provide feedback outside of class or during appropriate times within class. Eventually, the paraprofessional assumes a classroom-based support role while continuing to provide needed support to students with and without disabilities as they work together.

Reflecting on the Impact of Peer Supports

Regular reflection on how well the intervention is being implemented and impacting students is essential to making data-based educational decisions. A number of approaches can be drawn upon by educators to gauge the success of this support model. Classroom observations can be used to capture a number of different student outcomes, including the number and nature of interactions among students, the amount of time students remain in proximity, the types of support peers are providing, and the extent to which students are engaged academically (Carter et al., 2011; Jimenez, Browder, Spooner, & Dibiase, 2012). Paraprofessionals can be taught to use structured data collection sheets to collect data consistently and objectively.

In addition to conducting direct observations of academic and social behaviors, soliciting the views of key stakeholders (e.g., students with severe disabilities, peers, teachers, parents) can provide important insights into the acceptability, feasibility, and impact of peer support arrangements. Talk with students about which aspects of the peer support arrangement they like and dislike, how well they feel it is going, and their recommendations for further improving the intervention. Staff within the classroom can offer recommendations for strengthening peer-delivered supports and describe the broader impact on the classroom. Last, parents can be asked about any changes they notice at home, including social contacts outside of school or increased enthusiasm about attending school. All of this information should be used to make needed adjustments to the peer support arrangements.

Fostering Social Connections Beyond the Classroom

Although the primary goal of peer support arrangements is to increase social and academic participation within a particular class, steps can also be taken to encourage new relationships to extend beyond the classroom. Encouraging students to learn about one another's interests and preferred activities is a good place to start. When students discover the interests they have in common they may be more likely to pursue shared activities together outside of class or school. Discussing specific times throughout the week when students might get together is another way to facilitate broader social connections. For example, students might be encouraged to hang out during class breaks, at lunch, or during club activities as part of peer network (Carter et al., 2013). Finding times during less structured, noninstructional settings may help the student with a disability feel more a part of the social aspect of the school community.

Schools sometimes choose to also establish more formal, schoolwide peer support programs (e.g., peer buddy courses, peer mentoring, Best Buddies) as an avenue for increasing interaction opportunities, involving additional students throughout the school, and creating a more welcoming school culture. Although such programs can be designed in multiple ways (e.g., Hughes & Carter, 2008; Janney & Snell, 2006), common steps include (a) generating support from administrators and other school staff, (b) identifying core program elements, (c) recruiting and selecting peers, (d) offering training to students on their roles and responsibilities, (e) providing structured opportunities for students to interact with one another, and (f) establishing mechanisms for sustaining and expanding the program.

Implementation Considerations

Within the professional literature, peer-mediated interventions have been implemented in a wide variety of ways, in diverse school settings, and across the grade span. Similar to all interventions involving students with severe disabilities, peer support arrangements should be individually tailored to meet the needs of participating students. Peers working with students with complex communication needs, unique behavioral challenges, or other intensive needs may benefit from more focused training and ongoing assistance to support their classmates well. Similarly, some students may have more extensive social-related needs in a particular classroom, whereas others may have more intensive academic-related needs. In each case, the training and support peers receive should match these different emphases.

The grade levels of participating students may also be a relevant factor to consider. In secondary schools, the prevailing peer culture can be especially relevant when designing these arrangements. Adolescents often have strong preferences about with whom they spend time, peer interactions increasingly take place away from adults, and the receptivity of peers to these interventions may be influenced by what other students think. As the secondary curriculum increases in complexity, peer support arrangements may also place greater emphasis on the exchange of academic support than typically occurs in the earlier grades. In elementary schools, however, inclusive education is usually more widely practiced and students often attend multiple classes with the same cohort of classmates. Thus, students with severe disabilities may be known by more of their classmates and spend an extended amount of time with their peer supports.

Final Thoughts

Supporting students with severe disabilities to access the myriad social and learning opportunities existing within any school is an important aspect of providing a well-rounded educational experience. The absence of supportive relationships and friendships can have a substantial impact on the wellbeing of students with disabilities, yet prevailing adult-delivered support models can inadvertently hinder the development of strong social connections among students. Peer support arrangements offer a promising approach for improving the social and academic participation of students within inclusive classrooms and extracurricular activities. When thoughtfully planned and carefully implemented, such interventions hold promise to foster the sorts of social connections that can make school so enjoyable for young people.

At Devin's next IEP meeting, the team discussed possible pathways for helping him develop more social connections with peers at Columbia. His mom mentioned that Devin had enjoyed being involved in a peer buddy program in elementary school. Although the high school did not offer a similar peer partner program, the team decided to establish peer support arrangements in each of Devin's general education classes as a way of promoting shared learning opportunities and fostering new relationships.

Ms. DeStazio met with the American history teacher to identify a couple of students who might be interested in getting to know and working alongside Devin. Because they were interested in encouraging friendship development as well as class participation, they thought about which students shared Devin's interests in music or sports. Two juniors in the class, Stephan and Mason, immediately came to mind, and both readily accepted the invitation. In the meantime, Devin's special education teacher worked with the classroom teachers to develop a plan outlining how Devin would participate in class activities and receive support from both peers and adults.

Stephan, Mason, and Devin all met with Ms. DeStazio over two lunch periods to get to know one another and talk about how they would work together during American history class. Although Ms. DeStazio shared a number of initial ideas from the written plan, the students were also able generate a number of other creative ideas for how they might help one another during various class activities (e.g., whole class discussions, guest speakers, small-group projects, independent seatwork). The next day, seating arrangements were adjusted, and Devin sat right in the middle of the classroom at the same table as Stephan and Mason. Ms. DeStazio showed the peers some ideas for encouraging Devin to use his communication device and modeled how to respond when Devin tugged on their shirt sleeves or collars. Gradually, the peers began involving Devin on collaborative projects, sharing their class materials, encouraging his participation in class discussions, highlighting important ideas, introducing him to other students, helping him check his work, and offering positive feedback.

By the end of the semester, Devin, Mason, and Stephan were working together with very little direct support from Ms. DeStazio. Although she continued to make sure Devin was experiencing success in this history class, Ms. DeStazio also assisted the classroom teacher and other students who needed additional help. Moreover, she used some of her time in the classroom to collect data on Devin's IEP goal progress and class participation. Her findings were compelling: Not only had Devin become more on-task when working with his peers, he also interacted with a broader range of peers, used his communication device more frequently, and started walking to and from class with Mason. Perhaps most exciting to the planning team, however, was the fact that Devin now ate lunch with Stephan, Mason, and several other students in their peer group. Devin definitely felt he truly belonged Columbia High School.

References

Browder, D. M., & Spooner, F. H. (2011). *Teaching students with moderate and severe disabilities.* New York, NY: Guilford.

Carter, E. W., Asmus, J., Moss, C. K., Cooney, M., Weir, K., Vincent, L., ... Fesperman, E. (2013). Peer network strategies to foster social connections among adolescents with and without severe disabilities. *TEACHING Exceptional Children, 46*(2), 51–59.

Carter, E. W., Bottema-Beutel, K., & Brock, M. E. (2014). Social interactions and friendships. In M. Agran, F. Brown, C. Hughes, C. Quirk, & D. Ryndak (Eds.), *Equity and full participation for individuals with severe disabilities: A vision for the future.* Baltimore, MD: Brookes.

Carter, E. W., Cushing, L. S., & Kennedy, C. H. (2009). *Peer support strategies: Improving all students' social lives and learning.* Baltimore, MD: Brookes.

Carter, E. W., & Kennedy, C. H. (2006). Promoting access to the general curriculum using peer support strategies. *Research and Practice for Persons with Severe Disabilities, 31*, 284–292.

Carter, E. W., Moss, C. K., Hoffman, A., Chung, Y. C., & Sisco, L. (2011). Efficacy and social validity of peer support arrangements for adolescents with disabilities. *Exceptional Children, 78*, 107–125.

Carter, E. W., & Pesko, M. J. (2008). Social validity of peer interaction intervention strategies in high school classrooms: Effectiveness, feasibility, and actual use. *Exceptionality, 16*, 156–173. http://dx.doi.org/10.1080/09362830802198427

Carter, E. W., Sisco, L. G., Brown, L., Brickham, D., & Al-Khabbaz, Z. A. (2008). Peer interactions and academic engagement of youth with developmental disabilities in inclusive middle and high school classrooms. *American Journal on Mental Retardation, 113*, 479–494. http://dx.doi.org/10.1352/2008.113:479-494

Carter, E. W., Sisco, L. G., Chung, Y., & Stanton-Chapman, T. (2010). Peer interactions of students with intellectual disabilities and/or autism: A map of the intervention literature. *Research and Practice for Persons with Severe Disabilities, 35*, 63–79. http://dx.doi.org/10.2511/rpsd.35.3-4.63

Chung, Y., Carter, E. W., & Sisco, L. G. (2012). Social interaction of students with severe disabilities who use augmentative and alternative communication in inclusive classrooms. *American Journal on Intellectual and Developmental Disabilities, 117*, 349–367. http://dx.doi.org/10.1352/1944-7558-117.5.349

Copeland, S. R., Hughes, C., Carter, E. W., Guth, C., Presley, J. A., Williams, C. R., ...Fowler, S. E. (2004). Increasing access to general education: Perspectives of participants in a high school peer support program. *Remedial and Special Education, 26*, 342–352. http://dx.doi.org/10.1177/07419325040250060201

Cushing, L. S., Clark, N. M., Carter, E. W., & Kennedy, C. H. (2005). Access to the general education curriculum for students with severe disabilities: What it means and how to accomplish it. *TEACHING Exceptional Children, 38*(2), 6–13.

Cushing, L. S., & Kennedy, C. H. (1997). Academic effects on students without disabilities who serve as peer supports for students with disabilities in general education classrooms. *Journal of Applied Behavior Analysis, 30,* 139–152.

Feldman, E. K., & Matos, R. (2013). Training paraprofessionals to facilitate social interactions between children with autism and their typically developing peers. *Journal of Positive Behavior Interventions, 5,* 169–179. http://dx.doi.org/10.1177/1098300712457421

Giangreco, M. F., & Broer, S. M. (2007). School-based screening to determine overreliance on paraprofessionals. *Focus on Autism and Other Developmental Disabilities, 22,* 149–158. http://dx.doi.org/10.1177/10883576070220030201

Giangreco, M. F., Doyle, M. B., & Suter, J. C. (2012). Constructively responding to requests for paraprofessionals: We keep asking the wrong questions. *Remedial and Special Education, 33,* 362–373. http://dx.doi.org/10.1177/0741932511413472

Giangreco, M. F., Suter, J. C., & Doyle, M. B. (2010). Paraprofessionals in inclusive schools: A review of recent research. *Journal of Educational and Psychological Consultation, 20,* 41–57. http://dx.doi.org/10.1080/10474410903535356

Hughes, C., & Carter, E. W. (2008). *Peer buddy programs for successful secondary school inclusion.* Baltimore, MD: Brookes.

Jackson, L. B., Ryndak, D. L., & Wehmeyer, M. L. (2008/2009). The dynamic relationship between context, curriculum, and student learning: A case for inclusive education as a research-based practice. *Research and Practice for Persons with Severe Disabilities, 33/34,* 175–195. http://dx.doi.org/10.2511/rpsd.33.4.175

Janney, R., & Snell, M. E. (2006). *Social relationships and peer support* (2nd ed.). Baltimore, MD: Brookes.

Jimenez, B. A., Browder, D. M., Spooner, F., & Dibiase, W. (2012). Inclusive inquiry science using peer-mediated embedded instruction for students with moderate intellectual disability. *Exceptional Children, 78,* 301–317. http://dx.doi.org/10.1177/001440291207800303

Jorgensen, C., McSheehan, M., & Sonnenmeier, R. (2010). *The beyond access model: Promoting membership, participation, and learning for students with disabilities in the general education classroom.* Baltimore, MD: Brookes.

Katz, J., & Mirenda, P. (2002). Including students with developmental disabilities in general education classrooms: Social benefits. *International Journal of Special Education, 17,* 25–35.

McLeskey, J., Landers, E., Williamson, P., & Hoppey, D. (2012). Are we moving toward educating students with disabilities in less restrictive settings? *The Journal of Special Education, 46,* 131–140. http://dx.doi.org/10.1177/0022466910376670

Chapter 8

Let's Hang Out!
Facilitating Meaningful Recreation and Leisure
Sharon deFur, Juliet E. Hart Barnett, and Kristen Tarantino

Dave, a strong, 14-year-old teenager with autism spectrum disorder (ASD) and other developmental disabilities (DD), had limited recreation and leisure experiences, particularly with other teens. His family used to enjoy the beach, swimming, and boating, but they had not been able to participate in these activities since Dave was very young. His family admitted that their attempts to take him places, particularly with a group, frequently resulted in a meltdown that was physically and emotionally exhausting and publicly embarrassing. They wanted to find an activity that Dave could do and enjoy along with the family and with friends.

Dave's individualized education program (IEP) added recreation therapy as a related service; assessment revealed that water and swimming were interests of Dave's. Private one-on-one lessons with the therapist in a heated indoor pool worked well for Dave. He even jumped into the water wearing a life jacket and squealed with delight!

Dave's teacher wanted to take the next step and take the class swimming at the outdoor community pool. Although Dave's parents were worried about his safety, they agreed that they wanted him to be comfortable at the pool with a group of teens. They wanted him to learn to "hang out" with friends.

The pool was busy that day with lots of children and teens playing, diving into the water, and playing Marco Polo. Dave began to get agitated shortly after arrival, rocking back and forth and pacing. Dave refused to wear the life jacket because it was red and he wanted a blue one. Dave screamed, "Blue, blue, blue," and threw himself onto the ground. Other teens began to look at him and ask, "What's wrong with him?" Dave's assistant found a blue life jacket, which Dave wore, and he began to calm down.

They found a quieter corner of the pool, and Dave edged in, but then jumped out and yelled, "Cold!" He then sat on the edge splashing the water a little and smiling. Suddenly, the Marco Polo game got close to him, and he began to scream and flap his hands; next he jumped out of the pool and began running out the gate toward the busy parking lot. His teacher caught up just in time. The pool manager came to the teacher and said, "I don't think he belongs here."

Too often, families and service providers report experiences similar to the situation described for Dave and swimming. At the same time, recreation researchers assert that participating in recreation and leisure activities offers social and often therapeutic value for youth with ASD or other DD (Duvdevany & Arar, 2004; Kroeger, Schultz, & Newsom, 2007; Menear & Smith, 2008; Potvin, Prelock, & Snider, 2008; Potvin, Snider, Prelock, Kehayia, & Wood-Dauphinee, 2013), including raised quality of life (Kleinert, Miracle, & Sheppard-Jones, 2007; Kurt & Tekin-Iftar, 2008) and social acceptance, particularly as adolescence approaches (Dodd, Zabriskie, Widmer, & Eggett, 2009). Specifically, engaging in structured and unstructured recreational activities can improve overall perceptual-motor skills, balance, and coordination as well as basic athletic skills for individuals with varying disabilities (Etzel-Wise & Mears, 2004) and has been found to fill habilitative needs for youth with DD (Jerome, Frantino, & Sturmey, 2007). Although leisure activities have been found to contribute positively to the psychological, cognitive, physical, social, and linguistic development of all children (Cuhadar & Diken, 2011), youth with ASD or other DD who have taken part in recreational and leisure skills training increased their attention to task and displayed improvement in problem-solving and decision-making skills (American Therapeutic Recreation Association, n.d.) while also demonstrating a decline in self-stimulating, stereotypical, and self-abusive behavior (Yilmaz, Birkan, Konukman, & Agbuga, 2005). Moreover, participation in structured physical activities increases social interaction and friendships with typically developing peers as well as improves social and adaptive skills of youth with ASD or other DD (Auxter, Pyfer, & Huettig, 2005; Groft & Block, 2003).

Although most participants experience social, physical, and/or psychological benefits from participating in recreation and leisure pursuits, universally designed participation can mitigate some of the challenges typically associated with ASD or other DD. Poor cardiovascular fitness, obesity, or limited health knowledge have been observed in youth with ASD or other DD (Borremans, Rintala, & McCubbin, 2010), yet being physically active has a positive impact on physical health (Etzel-Wise & Mears, 2004). Although uncertain or limited friendships beset youth with ASD or other DD (Kaland, Mortensen, & Smith, 2011), recreation and leisure activities support the development of friendships, broaden interests, lessen feelings of loneliness, and promote involvement in the community (Duvdevany & Arar, 2004; McIntyre, Kraemer, Blacher, & Simmerman, 2004; Murphy & Carbone, 2008; Potvin et al., 2008; Potvin et al., 2013).

Moreover, meaningful and appropriately structured recreational activities strengthen self-determination skills, which include self-awareness, self-advocacy, goal setting, and problem solving/reframing to achieve goals (Wehmeyer & Field, 2007; Weymeyer et al., 2011). Direct instruction in self-determination skills or social skills to youth with varying disabilities continues as a viable base for self-determination basics, which have gained precedence as critical transition skills influencing postschool success for young adults with disabilities (Wehmeyer & Field, 2007; Wehmeyer et al., 2011). Experiences in recreational activities provide direct instruction and feedback regarding one's strengths and challenges and often ask participants to set and monitor goals, which can support participant choice by the adolescent with ASD or other DD (Wehmeyer & Field, 2007).

Arguably, adolescents and young adults with ASD or other DD continue to be described as having few friends, engaging in limited participation in organized or unorganized social interactions or recreation, and accessing a restricted range of integrated opportunities in spite of what we understand about the value of participating in recreation and leisure activities (Abells, Burbidge, & Minnes, 2008; Newman et al., 2011; Wagner, Cadwallader, & Marder, 2003; Orsmond,

Krauss, & Seltzer, 2004). Research suggests that youth with high functioning autism participate in a narrower range of physical activities or formal recreational activities than their same-age, typical peers; most commonly, these children's recreation or leisure activities take place in their own homes or the homes of relatives (Potvin et al., 2013). Correspondingly, Abells and colleagues (2008) reported that youth with intellectual disability (ID) spend only a small amount of time each week engaging in unorganized activities with peers, and most of the youths' social activities occur with family members. Notably, most of the youth who participated in organized recreational activities did so only through segregated programs (Abells et al., 2008).

Barriers to Recreation and Leisure for Youth With ASD or DD

Although there are specific characteristics associated with ASD and with DD, both disability classifications cover a broad range of intellectual and developmental skills (Turnbull, Turnbull, Wehmeyer, & Shogren, 2013). Nevertheless, having some or all of the disability characteristics can create barriers to full participation in leisure and recreational activities. For example, youth with ASD often have delays in expressive or receptive language development (Tager-Flusberg, Paul, & Lord, 2005), uneven intellectual development (Fombonne, 2005), and literal and concrete interpretations (Ozonoff & Miller, 1996) that challenge coaching or instruction in meaningful ways. Many of these youth have difficulty forming personal attachments (Thompson, 2007, 2008), which makes team participation difficult without adequate support. Common characteristics of youth with ASD are the need for sameness, difficulty with change or transitions, and a lack of spontaneity (Kim & Lord, 2010). Many recreational activities have a degree of unpredictability, which could elicit a negative reaction, such as a tantrum, from the youth (Brosnan & Healy, 2011). Youth with ASD may experience sensory and perceptual difficulties, including low muscle tone and awkward gait (Donnellan, Hill, & Leary, 2010); some engage in stereotypical or self-injurious behaviors that create barriers to social relationships (Symons, Byiers, Raspa, Bishop, & Bailey, 2010). In sum, youth with ASD have a varying range of functional independence (Patten, Baranek, Watson, & Schultz, 2013; Rosenberg, Westling, & McLeskey, 2011; Smith & Philippen, 2005).

Youth with DD also comprise a wide range of cognitive abilities, physical abilities, and functional independence (Rosenberg et al., 2011). Characteristics commonly associated with DD include a short attention span (Rosenberg et al., 2011; Sharpton & West, 2005), language delays (Targett & Langone, 2005), and poor memory (Turnbull et al., 2013), which would affect the ability to attend to and learn the rules of a game. Many youth with DD have both fine and gross motor delays as a result of neurological or physiological conditions that could interfere with being in an integrated sports recreational setting without the proper supports (Sharpton & West, 2005). Youth with DD may have limited problem-solving abilities, and, similar to youth with ASD, may not recognize social cues or threats, which can be exacerbated by placement in segregated activities (Rosenberg et al., 2011).

Youth participation in recreation and leisure activities depends on family involvement and support (Kleinert et al., 2007; Orsmond et al., 2004). However, families vary in their expectations for what youth with ASD or other DD can do in and out of school. Abells and colleagues (2008) found that parents of youth with ID credited the youth's disability as a primary reason for not participating in recreational activities with peers. In addition, families that are not heavily involved in the school or community may not be aware of their youth's friends at school, thus making it almost impossible to create organized peer events for their teens (deFur, Lee, Choi, & Rusniak, 2009).

Parents raise legitimate concerns associated with participation in a recreation or leisure program. First, parents of children with ASD or other DD may be hypersensitive about the safety of their children (deFur et al., 2009). For example, youth with ASD or other DD are often targets for bullying and for sexual abuse (Sharpton & West, 2005; Targett & Langone, 2005; Turnbull et al., 2013). Parents want to protect their children no matter what the circumstances, and, depending on the nature of the activity, there is a realistic fear that a child could be injured or worse. Because youth with ASD or other DD may have some communication difficulty, a second compounding fear for parents is that if something does happen, the youth might not be able to tell them (deFur et al., 2009).

Least Restrictive Environment for Recreational and Leisure Activities

Participation in both integrated and segregated recreational activities benefit youth with ASD or other DD, although the literature supports added social relationship benefits when the activities are integrated (American Therapeutic Recreation Association, n.d.; Duvdevany & Arar, 2004). For youth with ASD or other DD, it is important to identify both a continuum of supports and a continuum of activities with a goal of participating as independently as possible and in integrated settings where possible. Some individuals may start out in a segregated activity to develop a level of skill competency and familiarity before moving to an integrated activity. For example, because individuals with ASD and DD prefer routine, introducing a youth to a sports program, such as those offered through the YMCA, the Special Olympics, local parks and recreation programs, and so on, can be designed initially as individual or small group lessons, thus allowing youth the opportunity to learn the basic skills and routines associated with the sport or activity prior to introducing the youth to a group setting. Integrated activities support peer relationships with nondisabled peers and may also facilitate social skill development in a way that segregated activities do not. Kleinert and colleagues (2007) suggest a variety of options for creating opportunities for integrated recreational activities, including classes that include extracurricular activities as part of their requirements (e.g., band, drama, art), volunteer opportunities or classes held outside of school, and school-sponsored activities such as sports events, dances, and overnight trips. By participating in a continuum of segregated and integrated activities, youth have more opportunities to develop self-determination, relationships, and social skills that may be difficult to learn in academic programs. Table 8.1 highlights select national organizations, programs, and other resources to explore when searching for more information about a recreational program or developing supports for integrated participation.

Table 8.1
Recreational and Leisure Organizations for Individuals With ASD or Other DD

Organization	Description
Best Buddies International http://www.bestbuddies.org	International organization dedicated to pairing individuals with intellectual/developmental disabilities with nondisabled peers in one-to-one friendships.
Disabled Sports USA http://www.disabledsportsusa.org	Community sports, recreation, and educational programming for youth and adults with disabilities.
Draw4Free http://www.draw4free.com	Online or downloadable computer drawing program.
Easter Seals http://www.easterseals.com	Provides a range of service options for individuals with ASD and other disabilities. Easter Seals offers recreation and camping services that are barrier-free and accessible across the country.
Fishing Has No Boundaries http://www.fhnbinc.org	Organization designed to make fishing accessible to individuals with disabilities.
Let's Play http://www.letsplay.buffalo.edu	Online resource with tips for how to adapt and select toys based on disability.
National Center on Accessibility http://www.ncaonline.org	Access issues unique to parks and recreation programs and facilities.
National Center on Physical Activity and Disability http://www.ncpad.org	Directories of information and organizations related to physical activities for individual with disabilities.
PATH International http://www.pathintl.org	Professional Association of Therapeutic Horsemanship International provides equine-assisted activities and therapies for individuals with special needs.
Scratch http://www.scratch.mit.edu	Free animation and art program that allows users to program interactive stories and games.

Organization	Description
Special Olympics http://www.specialolympics.org	Offers information on year-round training and competition in Olympic-style sports, as well as coaching resources, for individuals with intellectual disabilities. Promotes unified sports for youth with and without disabilities. Includes resources for educators to create Project Unify in their schools.
Switch in Time http://www.switchintime.com	Accessible software, including computer games for individuals with disabilities.
Therapeutic Recreation Directory http://www.recreationtherapy.com	Clearinghouse of resources related to therapeutic recreation, including ideas for activities, links related to education, programs, therapeutic recreation, forums, and more.
United States Adaptive Recreation Center http://www.usarc.org	Offers adaptive programs across the United States in summer and winter Olympic-type sports.
YMCA http://www.ymca.net	Offers adaptive swimming lessons for children with special needs as well as other opportunities for recreation in an integrated setting.

Note. ASD = autism spectrum disorder, DD = developmental disabilities.

Strategies to Support Meaningful Participation in Recreational and Leisure Activities

Before addressing specific strategies to support youth with ASD or other DD, the IEP and transition planning process offers a natural venue for implementing a collaborative team approach for exploring recreational and leisure activities (deFur, 2009; Etzel-Wise & Mears, 2004; Kleinert et al., 2007; Menear & Smith, 2008; Potvin et al., 2008). For example, at the very least the IEP must address related services, transportation, and physical education, including adaptive physical education (Etzel-Wise & Mears, 2004), extracurricular activities, assistive technology, and the need for extended school year services. Of concern, particularly for youth with ASD or other DD, is the fact that independent living, including recreation and leisure, often receives less IEP attention (Chambers et al., 2007; deFur, Getzel, & Kregel, 1994; Potvin et al., 2008). Adult service agencies that might be providing or paying for transition services are included in transition planning;

these partners add other potential collaboration team members who offer support for recreational and leisure services. IEP teams (that include family and transition-age youth) have an annual opportunity to explore how leisure education or recreational activities can help youth with ASD or other DD achieve their goals for social skills, communication, behavior management, self-determination, and independent living.

Recreation as a "related service," according to the Individuals With Disabilities Education Act (2006), also includes therapeutic recreation services, leisure education, and recreation programs in schools and community agencies (34 C.F.R. § 300.34[c][11]). According to the National Dissemination Center for Children with Disabilities (2010), these services can be offered during or after the school day and in the community. Schools can partner with local parks and recreation programs or other youth recreational programs to increase the opportunities for integrated participation for youth with ASD or other DD. Educators, school therapists, and family members have unique knowledge and skills that can be shared with coaches or volunteers who lead community- or school-based leisure and recreational activities.

Youth with ASD or other DD vary in their needs for accommodations and supports to participate in recreational and leisure activities in integrated or segregated settings. A series of focused questions used collaboratively with IEP team members, including families and youth, can be a good starting point. Questions for reflection might include:

- What annual or transition outcome goals might be supported by participation in leisure and recreational activities?

- How might the youth's disability impact his or her participation in recreational and leisure activities?

- Have age-appropriate assessments of leisure and recreational interests and skills been completed?

- What are the leisure and recreational opportunities in the school, community, region, or state?

These exploration questions help the collaborative team discuss the importance of recreation and leisure in relation to the specific youth, consider barriers and plan strategies, discuss assessments, give choice to the youth and his or her family, and promote problem-solving. A continuum of recreational and leisure supports, including assistive technologies, can be identified based on student needs.

Unlike most typically developing peers, most youth with ASD or other DD need more explicit instruction in leisure education that generalizes to unstructured settings or more structured support for organized recreational and leisure activities, whether in integrated or segregated settings (Cuhadar & Diken, 2011). Lacking social skills necessary to completely participate in recreational and leisure programs can lead to self-imposed isolation. Instead of interacting *with* other youth, a child might play *around* other youth and remain locked in his or her own world. The key to a good recreational program aimed at encouraging social interaction is to provide structured interactions and supports so that a youth can be successful. Social interactions must be monitored and facilitated so that isolation does not become the primary choice of the youth. Schools have an ongoing opportunity to encourage and facilitate full participation in recreational and leisure activities for youth with ASD or other DD through implementation of research-based and easy-to-implement strategies as part of naturally occurring instructional routines (Hart & Whalon, 2008). Strategies to consider may be grouped by those that specifically target engaging family, peers, and community partners in order to provide students with the social skills needed to successfully engage in recreational and leisure activities.

Engage Families

Families are key to ongoing social participation as youth with ASD or other DD transition to adulthood. Families who are socially active influence their children to also be active (Orsmond et al., 2004), yet families often depend on schools or agencies to help form those networks (deFur et al., 2009). Families need information about the availability of opportunities as well as assurances that their sons or daughters can participate safely.

To engage families, create a space (whether online, on a bulletin board, or in a newsletter) that features upcoming opportunities for recreation and leisure; your students can help you with the link and maintaining the site. Send e-mails or newsletters; your students can help or take the lead on adding information about recreational and leisure opportunities that interest them. Create a class calendar and add important dates regarding school events, extracurricular opportunities, sports clubs, community events, and other opportunities. Have students create videos about their recreational and leisure interests and send it home to their families. Assign homework to find out what recreational and leisure events are happening for the next month and ask students to write or draw about their experience. Sponsor a family fun night for your class and ask sponsors of recreational and leisure activities (e.g., Special Olympics, Parks and Recreation) to speak at the event.

Develop Peer Partners

There are many formal and informal ways to promote friendships for teens with ASD or other DD in school, starting with a simple lunch buddy program involving typically developing peers at a critical hang out, the lunchroom. Start a Project Unify Club in your school using the resources from Special Olympics web site. Develop a mentor program by partnering with your local college or university or even a local sports team. Check out your nearest Independent Living Center, a federally funded agency that provides mentoring to youth with disabilities. Create your own e-mail pen pal program between your class and another class of typically developing students. Survey your school and look for matching interests regarding music, dance, or sports, and create an integrated club around that interest.

Employ Research-Based Practices

To experience success, youth with ASD or other DD often need direct instruction or other supports to prepare them to participate in these integrated events. Social stories for students with ASD or other DD have been shown to increase positive interactions with peer partners (Delano & Snell, 2006). Social stories are individualized stories that direct an individual on a particular behavior (Delano & Snell, 2006). This chapter's opening vignette introduced us to Dave, who may benefit from a social story on swimming at the pool with friends. Dave's teacher would first need to assess the particular behaviors that Dave would need to learn in order to interact positively with his peers at the local pool. A social story can also include important environmental and context clues that assist the student in knowing the appropriate time or place for a particular behavior. After a particular behavior is identified for the student, the teacher would create a short story that includes directive, descriptive, and affirmative statements about using that behavior as well as images that could aid in comprehension. Teachers should assist the student with reading and confirm comprehension of the story before allowing the student to practice the behavior in an applied, play setting (Delano & Snell, 2006). Repeated reading and practice sessions may be necessary to produce long-term maintenance of a learned behavior.

Practicing conversations and using video modeling to refine conversation and turn-taking skills can prepare youth for what to expect in the recreational setting (Johnson, Blood, Freeman, & Simmons, 2013). Similar to social stories, video modeling is a technique that teachers can use to demonstrate a particular behavior (Bellini & Akullian, 2007; Ganz, Earles-Vollrath, & Cook, 2011). For example, Dave's teacher may employ a video model that depicts a fellow student going to the pool, picking out a life vest, splashing in the water, and exhibiting enthusiasm in playing with peers. Videos can use peers and other individuals for models, or they can use a self-modeling approach in which the student would be videotaped performing the particular behaviors and shown the video as both a reminder and to reinforce the learned behaviors (Ganz et al., 2011. Implementing video modeling follows a step-by-step process that is similar to social story development and implementation. Teachers would need to identify the behavior to be featured, produce a video that demonstrates the behavior for the student to watch, check for comprehension, and allow the student the opportunity to apply the new behavior. See Delano and Stone's Chapter 4 of this volume for a step-by-step guide to video modeling.

Investigate Applications

Tablet or iPod applications that support communication or provide prompts for peer conversation are also a viable option to prepare students for the social interactions requisite for active participation in recreational activities. Applications such as iPrompts allow individuals to create visual schedules that include timers and pictures, which could encourage the youth to know what comes next and to be prepared for that next step. Conversation Builder is an iPad application that teaches children the main elements of having a conversation with a peer: introductions, changing the topic, sharing information, and so on. Such an application may be helpful for those youth who find it difficult to interact socially with peers. The Autism Speaks web site maintains a running list of applications that are potentially helpful for individuals with ASD or other DD. The featured applications are divided by the area that would be addressed, the appropriate age range, and whether or not research supports the effectiveness of the learning application. The price of each application is also identified on the web site. Visit http://www.autismspeaks.org/autism-apps for more information.

Collaborate With Community Partners

In your community, there are organizations and agencies that you can partner with to create or access recreational and leisure opportunities. You will have to do a little homework to create a community map of options for your students and identify people with whom you can partner.

Start with your local city or county web site, which will typically list county agencies such as Parks and Recreation. These agencies advertise activities and opportunities, either free or with a fee, as well as opportunities for services for individuals with disabilities. Conduct a web search for recreational opportunities for youth with ASD or other DD (see Table 8.1 as a starting place); you are likely to find links to a variety of web-based or downloadable resources. Smart-phones and tablets have applications for state and national parks, site seeing, and social networking. Offer to perform a community service either as a class or in partnership with typically developing youth. This could include volunteering at a home for the elderly, working on a habitat for humanity project, cleaning up a park, or helping with a preschool program. Giving students who are often served the opportunity to serve others is transformative in many ways.

Dave's IEP team reflected on Dave's experience at the community pool and decided that he needed instruction and scaffolding to assist his transition from structured private lessons to unstructured swimming settings. They decided to first move from private lessons to small group instruction with typically developing youth to provide peer interaction in the water and to assess Dave in a small group setting. His teacher, Ms. Lotts, began by developing a social story about swimming with friends that included pictures of the instructional pool, Dave, the swim instructor, and the friends who will join him. The story, titled "Swimming with Friends," included the following: Dave likes to play in the pool and learn to swim from Mr. Paulo. Dave's friends, Max and Carla, want to join Dave at the pool. Dave, Max, and Carla will swim and splash together. It will be fun!

The transition to the small group quickly met with success, even when Dave got splashed with water. Then Ms. Lotts and Mr. Paulo prepared for the community setting. Max, one of Dave's new pool friends, agreed to follow a script and be videotaped at the community pool filled with other noisy swimmers. Max narrated his action directing his comments directly to Dave. First, he put on a red life jacket, noting that it was a different color, but worked the same. Then, he put his foot in the edge of water, saying that the water was cold at first. He got all the way in the water and watched the Marco Polo game. Then, as some other swimmers came nearby, he kicked in the water and said how much fun he was having. The final video was only about 40 seconds long. Ms. Lotts showed the first 10 seconds of the video to Dave, then gradually showed the entire video. Dave watched the video each day for several days. The IEP team decided it was time to try the community pool again. Dave watched the video once more, and Max and Carla went with him to the pool along with his teachers. Although Dave was still a bit unsure about how cold the water was, he went in the pool that day, kicked and splashed, and laughed with his friends. The pool manager gave Dave a high five as he left the pool that day!

Final Thoughts

We hope this chapter has convinced you of the power of recreational and leisure activities to help youth with ASD or other DD hang out with friends. We urge you to help youth and families plan for lifelong participation in recreation and leisure to maintain physical fitness and community inclusion. Be proactive for your students or your youth, and allow yourself some time to participate in recreational and leisure activities too!

References

Abells, D., Burbidge, J., & Minnes, P. (2008). Involvement of adolescents with intellectual disabilities in social and recreational activities. *Journal on Developmental Disabilities, 14,* 88–94.

American Therapeutic Recreation Association. (n.d.). *Report on summary of outcomes.* Retrieved from http://atraonline.com/associations/10488/files/SummaryOutcomesTR.pdf

Auxter, D., Pyfer, J., & Huettig, C. (2005). *Principles and methods of adapted physical education and recreation* (10th ed.). Boston, MA: McGraw Hill.

Bellini, S., & Akullian, J. (2007). A meta-analysis of video modeling and video self-modeling interventions for children and adolescents with autism spectrum disorders. *Exceptional Children, 73,* 264–287. http://dx.doi.org/10.1177/001440290707300301

Borremans, E., Rintala, P., & McCubbin, J. A. (2010). Physical fitness and physical activity in adolescents with Asperger syndrome: A comparative study. *Adapted Physical Activity Quarterly, 27,* 308–320.

Brosnan, J., & Healy, O. (2011). A review of behavioral interventions for the treatment of aggression in individuals with developmental disabilities. *Research in Developmental Disabilities, 32,* 437–446. http://dx.doi.org/10.1016/j.ridd.2010.12.023

Chambers, C. R., Wehmeyer, M. L., Saito, Y., Lika, L. M., Lee, Y., & Singh, V. (2007). Self-determination: What do we know? Where do we go? *Exceptionality, 15,* 3–15. http://dx.doi.org/10.1080/09362830709336922

Cuhadar, S., & Diken, I. H. (2011). Effectiveness of instruction performed through activity schedules on leisure skills of children with autism. *Education and Training in Autism and Developmental Disabilities, 46,* 386–398.

deFur, S. H. (2009). Parents as collaborators: Building collaborative partnerships with school-based and community-based providers. In D. Wandry & A. Pleet (Eds.), *Engaging and empowering families in secondary transition – A practitioner's guide* (pp. 33–52). Arlington, VA: Council for Exceptional Children.

deFur, S., Getzel, E., & Kregel, J. (1994). Individual transition plans: A work in progress. *Journal of Vocational Rehabilitation, 4,* 139–145.

deFur, S. H., Lee, G., Choi, J., & Rusniak, K. (2009, Fall). *Recreation and leisure activities for youth with disabilities: What do families say?* Poster session presented at the Council for Exceptional Children International Division on Career Development and Transition Conference, Orlando, FL.

Delano, M., & Snell, M. E. (2006). The effects of social stories on the social engagement of children with autism. *Journal of Positive Behavior Interventions, 8,* 29–42. http://dx.doi.org/10.1177/1098300706080010501

Dodd, D., Zabriskie, R. B., Widmer, M. A., & Eggett, D. (2009). Contributions of family leisure to family functioning among families that include children with developmental disabilities. *Journal of Leisure Research, 41,* 261–286.

Donnellan, A. M., Hill, D. A., & Leary, M. R. (2010). Rethinking autism: Implications of sensory and movement differences. *Disability Studies Quarterly, 30,* 1–26.

Duvdevany, I., & Arar, E. (2004). Leisure activities, friendships, and quality of life of persons with intellectual ability: Foster homes vs. community residential settings. *International Journal of Rehabilitation Research, 27,* 289–296. http://dx.doi.org/10.1097/00004356-200412000-00006

Etzel-Wise, D., & Mears, B. (2004). Adapted physical education and therapeutic recreation in schools. *Intervention in School and Clinic, 39,* 223–232. http://dx.doi.org/10.1177/1053451204 0390040401

Fombonne, E. (2005). Epidemiology of autistic disorder and other pervasive developmental disorders. *Journal of Clinical Psychiatry, 66,* 3–8.

Ganz, J. B., Earles-Vollrath, T. L., & Cook, K. E. (2011). Video modeling: A visually based intervention for children with autism spectrum disorder. *TEACHING Exceptional Children, 43*(6), 8–19.

Groft, M., & Block, M. (2003). Children with Asperger syndrome: Implications for general physical education and youth sports. *Journal of Physical Education, Recreation and Dance, 74*(3), 38–43. http://dx.doi.org/10.1080/07303084.2003.10608468

Hart, J. E., & Whalon, K. J. (2008). Promote academic engagement and communication of children with autism spectrum disorder in inclusive settings. *Intervention in School and Clinic, 44,* 116–120.

IDEA regulations, 34 C.F.R. § 300 (2012).

Individuals With Disabilities Education Act, 20 U.S.C. §§ 1400 *et seq.* (2006 & Supp. V. 2011)

Jerome, J., Frantino, E. P., & Sturmey, P. (2007). The effects of errorless learning and backward chaining on the acquisition of Internet skills in adults with developmental disabilities. *Journal of Applied Behavior Analysis, 40,* 185–189. http://dx.doi.org/10.1901/jaba.2007.41-06

Johnson, J. W., Blood, E., Freeman, A., & Simmons, K. (2013). Evaluating the effectiveness of teacher-implemented video prompting on an iPod touch to teach food-preparation skills to high school students with autism spectrum disorders. *Focus on Autism and Other Developmental Disabilities, 28,* 147–158. http://dx.doi.org/10.1177/1088357613476344

Kaland, N., Mortensen, E. L., & Smith, L. (2011). Social communication impairments in children and adolescents with Asperger syndrome: Slow response time and the impact of prompting. *Research in Autism Spectrum Disorders, 5,* 1129–1137. http://dx.doi.org/10.1016/j.rasd.2010.12.009

Kim, S. H., & Lord, C. (2010). Restricted and repetitive behaviors in toddlers and preschoolers with autism spectrum disorders based on the autism diagnostic observation schedule (ADOS). *Autism Research, 3,* 162–173. http://dx.doi.org/10.1002/aur.142

Kleinert, H. L., Miracle, S. A., & Sheppard-Jones, K. (2007). Including students with moderate and severe disabilities in extracurricular and community recreation activities. *TEACHING Exceptional Children, 39*(6), 33–38.

Kroeger, K. A., Schultz, J. R., & Newsom, C. (2007). A comparison of two group-delivered social skills programs for young children with autism. *Journal of Autism and Developmental Disorders, 37,* 808–817. http://dx.doi.org/10.1007/s10803-006-0207-x

Kurt, O., & Tekin-Iftar, E. (2008). A comparison of constant time delay and simultaneous prompting within embedded instruction on teaching leisure skills to children with autism. *Topics in Early Childhood Special Education, 28*, 53–64. http://dx.doi.org/10.1177/0271121408316046

McIntyre, L., Kraemer, B., Blacher, J., & Simmerman, S. (2004). Quality of life for young adults with severe intellectual disability: Mothers' thoughts and reflections. *Journal of Intellectual and Developmental Disability, 29*, 131–146. http://dx.doi.org/10.1080/13668250410001709485

Menear, K. S., & Smith, S. (2008). Physical education for students with autism. *TEACHING Exceptional Children, 40*(5), 32–37.

Murphy, N., & Carbone, P. (2008). Promoting the participation of children with disabilities in sports, recreation, and physical activities. *Pediatrics, 121*, 1057–1061. http://dx.doi.org/10.1542/peds.2008-0566

National Dissemination Center for Children with Disabilities (NICHCY). (2010). *Contents of the IEP.* Retrieved from http://nichcy.org/schoolage/iep/iepcontents

Newman, L., Wagner, M., Knokey, A.-M., Marder, C., Nagle, K., Shaver, D., & Wei, X. (2011). *The post-high school outcomes of young adults with disabilities up to 8 years after high school. A report from the National Longitudinal Transition Study-2* (NLTS2; Report No. NCSER 2011-3005). Menlo Park, CA: SRI International.

Orsmond, G. I., Krauss, M. W., & Seltzer, M. M. (2004). Peer relationships and social and recreational activities among adolescents and adults with autism. *Journal of Autism and Developmental Disorders, 43*, 246–256. http://dx.doi.org/10.1023/b:jadd.0000029547.96610.df

Ozonoff, S., & Miller, J. N. (1996). An exploration of right-hemisphere contributions to the pragmatic impairments of autism. *Brain and Language, 52*, 411–434. http://dx.doi.org/10.1006/brln.1996.0022

Patten, E., Baranek, G. T., Watson, L. R., & Schultz, B. (2013). Child and family characteristics influencing intervention choices in autism spectrum disorders. *Focus on Autism and Other Developmental Disabilities, 28*, 138–146. http://dx.doi.org/10.1177/1088357612468028

Potvin, M. C., Prelock, P. A., & Snider, L. (2008). Collaborating to support meaningful participation in recreational activities of children with autism spectrum disorder. *Topics in Language Disorders, 28*, 365–374. http://dx.doi.org/10.1097/01.tld.0000341129.01158.bb

Potvin, M. C., Snider, L., Prelock, P., Kehayia, E., & Wood-Dauphinee, S. (2013). Recreational participation of children with high functioning autism. *Journal of Autism and Developmental Disorders, 43*, 445–457. http://dx.doi.org/10.1007/s10803-012-1589-6

Rosenberg, M. S., Westling, D. L., & McLeskey, J. (2011). *Special education for today's teachers: An introduction.* Upper Saddle River, NJ: Pearson Education.

Sharpton, W. R., & West, M. D. (2005). Severe intellectual disability. In P. Wehman, P. J. McLaughlin, & T. Wehman (Eds.), *Intellectual and developmental disabilities: Toward full community inclusion* (3rd ed., pp. 219–240). Austin, TX: PRO-ED.

Smith, M. D., & Philippen, L. (2005). Autism. In P. Wehman, P. J. McLaughlin, & T. Wehman (Eds.), *Intellectual and developmental disabilities: Toward full community inclusion* (3rd ed., pp. 309–355). Austin, TX: PRO-ED.

Symons, F. J., Byiers, B. J., Raspa, M., Bishop, E., & Bailey, D. B. (2010). Self-injurious behavior and fragile X syndrome: Findings from the national fragile X survey. *American Association on Intellectual and Developmental Disabilities, 115*, 473–481. http://dx.doi.org/10.1352/1944-7558-115.6.473

Tager-Flusberg, H., Paul, R., & Lord, C. (2005). Language and communication in autism. In F. R. Volkmar, R. Paul, A. Klin, & D. Cohen (Eds.), *Handbook of autism and pervasive developmental disorders* (3rd ed., pp. 335–364). New York, NY: Wiley.

Targett, P., & Langone, J. (2005). Mild intellectual disability. In P. Wehman, P. J. McLaughlin, & T. Wehman (Eds.), *Intellectual and developmental disabilities: Toward full community inclusion* (3rd ed., pp. 189–217). Austin, TX: PRO-ED.

Thompson, T. (2007). *Making sense of autism.* Baltimore, MD: Brookes.

Thompson, T. (2008). *Dr. Thompson's straight talk on autism.* Baltimore, MD: Brookes.

Turnbull, A., Turnbull, H. R., Wehmeyer, M. L., & Shogren, K. A. (2013). *Exceptional lives: Special education in today's schools* (7th ed.). Upper Saddle River, NJ: Pearson.

Wagner, M., Cadwallader, T. W., & Marder, C. (with Cameto, R., Cardoso, D., Garsa, N., Levine, P., & Newman, L.). (2003). *Life outside the classroom for youth with disabilities: A report from the National Longitudinal Transition Study-1 (NLTS2).* Menlo Park, CA: SRI International. Retrieved from http://www.nlts2.org/reports/2003_04-1/nlts2_report_2003_04-2_complete.pdf

Wehmeyer, M. L., & Field, S. L. (2007). *Self-determination: Instructional and assessment strategies.* Thousand Oaks, CA: Corwin.

Wehmeyer, M. L., Palmer, S. B., Williams-Diehm, K., Shogren, K. A., Davies, D. K., & Stock, S. (2011). Technology and self-determination in transition planning: The impact of technology use in transition planning on student self-determination. *Journal of Special Education Technology, 26*(1), 13–24.

Yilmaz, Y., Birkan, B., Konukman, F., & Agbuga, B. (2005). Effects of progressive time delay method on teaching basic progression swimming skills for children with autism. *Research Quarterly for Exercise and Sport, 76,* A119–A120.

Chapter 9

Let's Talk About Sex: Promoting Healthy Relationships and Sexuality

Peggy Schaefer Whitby and Jason Travers

Sara is a 15-year-old girl with intellectual disability. Similar to most 15-year-old girls, Sara desperately wants a boyfriend. She is a very attractive and naïve young lady. She recently has started to act on her crushes. Sara follows the boy she has a crush on, tells others he is her boyfriend, and writes love letters to him. The boys do not always have the same feelings for her, but Sara continues her pursuit until she has a crush on a different boy. Sara participated in the ninth-grade health-education class and a social-skills group. However, her parents are concerned about her ability to implement her knowledge in a real-world setting. They are concerned she will be teased, or worse, sexually exploited.

Sara's parents want her to have meaningful intimate relationships, but they are worried for her safety. Although the thought of Sara getting hurt or pregnant frightens her parents, they realize that Sara has normal desires and a right to have intimate relationships. They discuss their concerns and risks with the individualized education program (IEP) team. To reduce the risks, the IEP team designs an intervention plan targeting appropriate skills for having a girlfriend or boyfriend. After assessing Sara's current level of social and relationship skills, it is determined that she needs to learn how to initiate appropriate social interactions with boys, read their social cues to determine if they are interested, and adjust her behavior accordingly.

Sexual development is an essential part of the human experience, but people with developmental disabilities (DD) have historically been viewed as sexually immature or entirely asexual (Konstantareas & Lunsky, 1997; Lesseliers & Van Hove, 2002; Stokes & Kaur, 2005). Human sexuality involves a person's development of their own beliefs, attitudes, values, sexual knowledge, and behavior as they relate to gender, other roles, identity, and personality (National Commission on Adolescent Sexual Health, 1995). Unfortunately, sex education may often be excluded from intervention programming for students with DD. A narrow view of sexuality, the taboo nature of sexuality, and laws regarding sex education may deter stakeholders from considering and providing sex education to students with DD (Travers & Tincani, 2010). However, this is problematic and may be counterproductive to achieving educational goals.

Sex education for students with DD is justified by at least four reasons: (a) to prevent sexual abuse, (b) to support the development of interpersonal relationships, (c) to prevent challenging behavior, and (d) to promote self-determination (Travers & Tincani, 2010; Travers, Tincani, Whitby, & Boutot, in press; Travers & Whitby, in press). Students with DD are at increased risk of sexual abuse. This may be because they often have limited communication skills that prevent them from reporting abuse (Mansell, Sobsey, & Moskal, 1998). Students with DD may not report sexual abuse because they simply are not aware that it is wrong. This means that the sex offender remains free to continue the abuse. Further, the emotional and physical impact on victims of sexual abuse who also have a DD can cause poor educational progress in social, behavioral, communicative, and academic areas. Although preventing abuse is important, it is not the only reason sex education is critical for learners with DD.

Students with DD are entitled to grow into adults with meaningful relationships. Friendship and companionship are essential to human development and happiness. Students with DD must be provided with early and ongoing supports that enhance their ability to live fulfilling lives as adults who can, to the greatest extent possible, engage in independent and/or consensual sexual behavior, choose and marry a life partner, and experience parenthood. Failure to address the social desires of students with DD may not only limit quality of life by diminishing the quality and quantity of their relationships but also may lead to increased inappropriate social and sexual behavior (e.g., public disrobing, public masturbation, touching other people; Ray, Marks, & Bray-Garretson, 2004; Stokes & Kaur, 2005). It is likely that inappropriate sexual behavior by a student with a disability is the reason why education teams begin considering sex education, but a reactive approach to inappropriate behavior is not ideal. A proactive approach leads to interventions and supports necessary for broader, healthy sexual development. Thus, sex education is necessary for promoting the development of various relationships as well as preventing challenging behavior associated with negative outcomes (Travers & Tincani, 2010).

Travers et al. (in press) suggested that sex education is compatible with, and perhaps necessary for, achieving greater self-determination. Self-determination has to do with the person's capacity, opportunities, and self-perceptions to independently make decisions about his or her life (Wehmeyer, 2001; Wehmeyer & Garner, 2003). Sex education can only enhance these aspects of self-determination and therefore has direct implications for quality of life. If students with DD are provided with ongoing and comprehensive sex education, they will be more likely to be safe from sexual abuse, have enriching relationships, demonstrate behavior consistent with social norms, and attain higher levels of self-determination. The purpose of this chapter is to provide a framework to teach sex education under the topics of social skills and health education.

Sex education is offered in public schools in many states, and children with DD who have parental consent can participate in the general education curriculum. However, participation does not guarantee student learning because some states have laws that prohibit comprehensive sex education (e.g., law may only allow for hygiene instruction). What follows are potentially effective strategies for individualized sex education for learners with DD. Although there exists very little empirical literature on interventions specific to sex education (Travers et al., in press), this chapter relies on methods that have been proven effective for teaching a variety of skills to learners with DD. Table 9.1 provides an overview of a framework for providing sex education for people with DD. Practitioners will need to investigate their state and local laws as well as school district policies regarding sex education before seeking permission from parents and providing instruction related to sexuality. Practitioners may consider using a sex education curriculum specifically designed for learners with DD to aid in the delivery of specialized instruction on sexuality. Table 9.2 draws from the Sexuality Information Education Center of the United States (SIECUS; 2004) to provide examples of standards to teach in order to build capacity and ideas to support opportunities for people with DD across the lifespan.

Table 9.1
Framework for Teaching Sex Education in School

Type of instruction	Components
Basic health education course	• Typical/general education course • Covers hygiene, sexuality, sexual health, and relationships • Students with DD can be included based upon their needs
Specialized sex education instruction	• Specific to people with DD • Can be paired with the basic health education course • Provides explicit instruction, either small group or individually
Individualized education program	• Develop individualized target behaviors and goals • Identifies evidence-based strategies to use during instruction • Aligned with the Sexuality Information Education Center of the United States guidelines for comprehensive sex education
Ongoing opportunities	• Social opportunities to develop relationships • Privacy to engage in appropriate sexual behavior consistent with person's capacity • Provide opportunities, enhance capacity, and promote self-perception for self-determination

Note. DD = developmental disabilities.

Age range	Developing the capacity	Supporting opportunities
Ages 5–11	• Social skills • Self-care and hygiene • Abuse prevention • Privacy and personal space • Body parts and puberty • Inappropriate touch • Use materials that are conducive to learning (Blanchett & Wolfe, 2002): For example, visuals, increased practice opportunities, modeling.	• Provide opportunities to build relationships with peers with and without disabilities (Bernert, 2011). • Promote decision-making (e.g., who to sit with at lunch, choosing quality friends; Swango-Wilson, 2011). • Use appropriate terminology. • Involve PWD in self-care and hygiene • Provide a means to communicate abuse, requests for privacy, or violations of personal space. • Take reports of abuse seriously (reports often are dismissed; Bernert, 2011). • Allow private time and develop policies for private time in group living situations (Bernert, 2011) with input from the consumers (Hollomotz & The Speakup Committee (2008). • Respect the personal space of PWD.

Note. PWD = People with disabilities.

Table 9.2 *(continued)*
Teaching Sex Education and Creating Opportunities Across the Lifespan

Age range	Developing the capacity	Supporting opportunities
Ages 12–18	• Social skills: dating and friendship • Sexual relationships, including the difference between healthy and unhealthy relationships • What is abuse or exploitation • Sexuality: gender, orientation • Adolescent physical development • Hygiene • Menstruation • Teach the "when, where, and how" of masturbation so that PWD do not act inappropriately or illegally • Privacy and personal space	• Include PWD so they can develop personal relationships (Bernert, 2011) • Support the desire to date and develop intimate relationships • Provide support for PWD to participate the greatest extent possible in self-care related to sexual health (e.g., breast examinations). • Develop appropriate privacy guidelines for settings and support the use of private time • Provide feedback regarding appropriate and inappropriate touching. Tell PWD what to do instead of what not to do • Provide a means to communicate relationship development, abuse, requests for privacy, or violations of personal space • Support PWD to act in an manner to prevent sexually transmitted diseases and pregnancy

Table 9.2 *(continued)*
Teaching Sex Education and Creating Opportunities Across the Lifespan

Age range	Developing the capacity	Supporting opportunities
Ages 18+	• Social skills: developing intimate, long-term relationships • Sexual relationships: boyfriends/girlfriends and husbands/wives • Preventing pregnancy • Sexual responsibilities • Family responsibilities	• Support the self-advocacy of PWD in the development of intimate relationships • Trust that PWD can learn and implement appropriate sexual practices • Develop living situations where PWD can develop relationships

Sex Education Curricula

Individualized education program teams should work together to identify what should be taught about sexuality and who will teach it (Travers & Tincani, 2010). However, decisions regarding curricula will require a basic understanding of comprehensive sex education. SIECUS has provided a guide, *Guidelines for Comprehensive Sex Education* (3rd ed.; 2004), that details all components of human sexual development. This extensive guide includes an outline of six key concepts of sexuality: human development, relationships, personal skills, sexual behavior, sexual health, and society and culture. Each concept contains "life behaviors" as well as related subconcepts. SIECUS provides standards across the life span, a list of available curricula, and lesson plans for teaching sexuality topics (see resources at http://www.siecus.org). The SIECUS document also provides guidelines for evaluating sex education curriculum manuals. IEP team members who are responsible for decisions related to sex education need to be critical consumers of curricula and should evaluate manuals before using them to deliver sex education to students with DD. Ideally, selected curricula will address sexuality across the lifespan as it relates to social development, human development, sexual health and hygiene, and sexual behavior. Social development instruction should emphasize both self-protection and promotion of various kinds of relationships. Close evaluation using the SIECUS curriculum-evaluation tool will reveal whether the curriculum contains adequate information to teach sex education. Table 9.3 lists some resources for sex education curricula; IEP teams will need to review and evaluate the resources not only to ensure they provide accurate and comprehensive information but also to ensure that the content and suggested instructional methods align with their values and other educational materials.

Table 9.3
Example Curricula for Teaching Sex Education to People With Developmental Disabilities

Age range	Sample curricula
Ages 5–11	• *Promoting Social Success: A Curriculum for Children with Special Needs* (Siperstein & Paige, 2004). • *Teaching Children with Down syndrome about Their Bodies, Boundaries and Sexuality: A Guide for Parents and Professionals* (Couwenhoven, 2007). www.woodbinehouse.com
Ages 12–18	• *Life Horizons I & II* (Kempton, 2005). www.stanfield.com • *Sex Education for Persons with Severe Developmental Disabilities* (Brekke, 1988). www.stanfield.com • *Taking Care of Myself: A Hygiene, Puberty and Personal Curriculum for Young People with Autism* (Wrobel, 2003). www.futurehorizons-autism.com
Ages 18+	• *Circles I: Intimacy and Relationships* (Walker-Hirsch, 2007). www.stanfield.com • *Relationship Series* (Young Adult Institute, 2013). www.yai.org • *Finger Tips: Teaching Women with Disabilities About Masturbation Through Understanding and Video* (Hingsburger & Haar, 2000). www.diverse-city.com • *Hand Made Love: A Guide for Teaching About Male Masturbation Through Understanding and Video* (Hingsburger, 2000). www.diverse-city.com

Individualizing Sex Education

Sexuality can be a very sensitive topic for families, but collaboration with parents is critical for sex education. Generally, parents give consent for their children, whether they have specialized needs or not, to participate in school-based sex education. People with DD have difficulty generalizing learning. Small-group or isolated instruction may not be enough, especially because these individuals need to learn natural cues in the environment. Achieving generalized learning requires collaboration with parents to develop and deliver supports across settings. By using the SIECUS standards to guide instruction, the IEP team can maintain a professional role while developing goals that reflect the family's (or person's) values.

People with DD will require specialized instruction that considers their strengths, weaknesses, preferences, and interests. Instruction is largely rooted in the field of behavior analysis. Behavior-analytic interventions include, but are not limited to, task analysis, prompting procedures, priming, reinforcement, shaping, and response interruption/redirection. Parents and professionals looking for additional information about applied behavior analysis techniques should consider the autism spectrum disorder Internet modules developed by the Ohio Center for Autism and Low Incidence (2013)(http://www.autisminternetmodules.org), the National Professional Development Center on Autism Spectrum Disorders (http://autismpdc.fpg.unc.edu/), or the Kansas University Center on Developmental Disabilities (http://www2.ku.edu/~kucdd/index.shtml).

Applied Behavior Analysis Strategies

The primary goal of applied behavior analysis is to support socially significant changes in behavior that enhance quality of life. Behavior analytic strategies begin with a definition of behavior that uses specific, observable, and measurable terms (Alberto & Troutman, 2009). One or several intervention strategies are then used to promote behavior change. Data are collected to evaluate the effects of the intervention of the defined behavior and, in accordance with the findings, intervention continues or is modified to achieve the desired change. One common and effective technique for changing behavior is the task analysis. Task analysis has been successfully used to teach a variety of skills (Franzone, 2009). The teaching process begins by breaking down a complex, multistep task into smaller, more manageable steps. The teacher then proceeds by systematically teaching one step of the behavior while also requiring independent performance of previously mastered steps. In some cases, the teacher will focus on student mastery of the first step (i.e., forward chaining), but often times it may be more effective to teach the last step first, then gradually teach each previous step (i.e., backward chaining). The reinforcing consequence for each step is (a) the completion of the step, (b) advancement to the next step, and, ultimately, (c) the completion of the final step (e.g., completing the task may result in a rewarding consequence, such as praise or preferred activity, escape from discomfort, or various combinations of both). In some cases, other rewards may initially be necessary to encourage completion of the steps and behaviors. Over time, additional rewards are reduced and, if possible, eliminated. With regard to sex education, task analysis may be used to teach an array of different skills, such as toileting routines, menstrual care, or contraception use (See Figure 9.1 for an example of a task analysis for menstrual care).

Prompts are additional cues given to a person to help that person recognize natural cues or perform a behavior (Neitzel & Wolery, 2009). The types of prompts used can vary from minimally intrusive (e.g., photographs/images, gestures) to highly intrusive (e.g., full physical support). Given that many people with DD have difficulty picking up on nuanced cues, especially social cues, prompts may be an effective way to support sex education. However, prompts must quickly be faded to the natural cue in order to avoid prompt dependence and learned helplessness. For example, students can use a cue card that includes scripts of appropriate responses to spoken greetings from peers paired with verbal prompts to get the card, look at it, read it aloud, and put it away. Over time, as the student recognizes the spoken greeting as the cue to respond, the cue card is faded because they no longer need the card to appropriately respond. Without fading the prompt (verbal prompts and cue cards), the student may indefinitely be dependent on another person to tell him or her what to do or say.

Figure 9.1
Task Analysis Menstruation Care

1	Go get new pad from _____.
2	Put pad in your pants pocket.
3	Go to the bathroom.
4	Go into bathroom stall.
5	Shut door.
6	Pull down pants.
7	If old pad is red or brown, take old pad off underwear.
8	Roll old pad and wrap with toilet paper.
9	Put old pad in trashcan.
10	Take new pad out of your pocket.
11	Take wrapper off new pad.
12	Unfold pad.
13	Pull paper strip off back of pad.
14	Place sticky side of pad on underwear.
15	Throw pad wrapper in trashcan.
16	Pull up pants.
17	Leave bathroom stall.
18	Wash hands.

Behaviors that occur are reinforced in the environment, and behaviors that do not occur are not reinforced in the environment (Cooper, Heron, & Heward, 2007). Teams need to ensure their interventions promote behaviors that have functional value in the natural environments where behaviors are expected to occur. When natural consequences act as reinforcement for behavior, then generalized learning has occurred. Further, students who are not responding in an expected or desirable way have not experienced reinforcing consequences for their appropriate behavior. Although rewards may be useful for supporting appropriate sociosexual interactions, natural reinforcers (e.g., gaining peer attention) will be necessary for maintaining and generalizing appropriate behavior.

Recruiting natural reinforcers may be difficult or seemingly impossible for promoting appropriate peer interactions for students who use inappropriate behavior to escape the attention of others (e.g., hitting, yelling). In these cases, a clear purpose of inappropriate behavior should be identified via functional assessment. Once a function is identified, interventions can focus on replacing inappropriate behavior with a more socially acceptable behavior. For example, a student with developmental disability may throw objects at people to make them go away (i.e., escape attention). A long-term goal would be to teach the person to deliver compliments in order to get the attention of others. However, the short-term objective is to replace object-throwing by teaching the person to tell others to go away (i.e., escape attention). Similarly, the function of Sara's behavior is to get the attention of boys she likes. Ideally, because of the natural consequence (embarrassment), Sara would leave alone boys who are unreceptive to her advances. Immediate interventions should emphasize broadening Sara's social skills and opportunities so that she can obtain attention of others using socially appropriate behaviors currently not in her repertoire. Preventing inappropriate reactions or using punishing consequences likely will not be effective because they (a) do not address the underlying skill deficit, (b) do not eliminate the person's need(s)/desire(s), and (c) require constant supervision with the threat of punishment (e.g., loss of privilege, additional chores).

Priming

Priming is an antecedent-based strategy that can be used to teach various social skills to people with DD (Koegel, Koegel, Frea, & Green-Hopkins, 2003; Zanolli, Daggett, & Adams, 1996). Priming involves the delivery of information about an expected behavior prior to the person's use of the behavior. In most cases, the information is presented via video or some other media so that the student "previews" the expectations, thus making the events more predictable (Schreibman, Whalen, & Stahmer, 2000). Priming can be used as a strategy to explicitly teach new behaviors or to promote generalization of already mastered skills. There are various methods for priming behavior in students with DD, including social stories (Gray, 2000) and other forms of social scripts, and video modeling (Bellini, 2008). These are examples of antecedent-based interventions that when delivered as a prime can be used to teach sex education.

Social stories (Gray, 2000) are individualized stories that assist children with DD in interpreting and understanding social situations. Social stories follow a specific format and formula of different sentence types. They are written to provide the student an understanding of what people do, think, or feel in a certain situation. More generally, social scripts and narratives serve a similar purpose and are less rigid in their design. The purpose is to enhance student understanding of social situations as well as guide their use of appropriate responses. Research suggests that social narratives are effective for increasing social communication, attention, and organizational skills of children with DD (Sansosti, Powell-Smith, & Kincaid, 2004). Social narratives also have been effective for supporting skills related to human sexuality (e.g., relationships, menstrual care, masturbation; Klett & Turan, 2011; Stefanos, Maria, & Elias, 2011; Tarnai & Wolfe, 2008). Figure 9.2 presents a sample social narrative on supporting students in differentiating friendships from romantic relationships.

Students with autism spectrum disorder (ASD) or other DD benefit from primes that are presented via video modeling (Bellini, 2008; Franzone & Collet-Klingenberg, 2008). Video modeling requires the creation of videos that use peers (i.e., peer video modeling) or the actual person (i.e., video self-modeling) completing the task or behavior. Video modeling has been used to teach functional skills (Mechling & Ayres, 2012; Rosenberg, Schwartz, & Davis, 2010) and help students learn conversational and interpersonal skills (Kagohara et al., 2013; Shukla-Mehta, Miller, & Callahan, 2010). Video modeling can be used to teach various skills related to sexuality, including hygiene (e.g., brushing teeth), sexual behavior (e.g., masturbation), and relationships (e.g., making friends, intimacy). A video-based curriculum for teaching about masturbation is commercially available for parents of young men (Hingsburger, 2000) and women (Hingsburger & Haar, 2000) with DD.

Figure 9.2
Social Story on Developing a Boyfriend/Girlfriend Relationship

---

Boyfriends and Boy Friends

Sometimes I may like a boy who looks handsome and is nice to me.
I may want to hold his hand or kiss him.

Before I can kiss him and hold his hand, I will to talk to him to find out if he likes me.
I can ask him what his name is. I can ask him what music he likes and what he likes to do for fun.

I will tell him what music I like and what my favorite movies are.
After we talk a few times, I can ask him if he has a girlfriend.

If he has a girlfriend, then we can only be friends.
We won't hold hands or kiss.

If he doesn't have a girlfriend, then he might ask me to go out to eat or see a movie.
We might hold hands and kiss, but only if we both want to.

Next time I see a handsome boy at school, I can talk to him to find out if he likes me.

Where a behavior occurs is the key factor in classifying it as appropriate or inappropriate (Sweeney, 2007). People with DD may make contextual errors regarding sexual behaviors. This means that teachers and parents will need to understand how to respond if an inappropriate behavior occurs. Response interruption/redirection (Neitzel, 2010) is an evidence-based strategy that may be helpful for addressing self-stimulatory behaviors (e.g., touching genitals or public masturbation). The strategy requires blocking the student's ability to engage in the behavior, immediately directing the student to an appropriate activity or behavior, and reinforcing the appropriate behavior. For example, if a student with a developmental disability attempts to disrobe in public, the supporting adult could block disrobing by moving the person's hands away from his or her clothing, ask the person to engage in a simple behavior that involves use of his or her hands (e.g., "pick up the book" or "push the cart"), then reinforce appropriate engagement for following the directions. The activity the student is directed to should engage the use of his or her hands and cognitive skills. Given the assumption that all behavior is learned and has a purpose, response interruption/redirection should be used in conjunction with other interventions and supports to enable the person to appropriately meet his or her sexual needs. For example, response interruption/redirection might be more effective for addressing inappropriate masturbation when additional interventions are used to ensure that the student learns that his or her bedroom is the only appropriate place to masturbate. Teaching the use of a bathroom to masturbate is discouraged because many bathrooms are not private and may result in abuse, arrest, and conviction of sexual crimes, or contribute to stigmatic notions that people with DD are sexually deviant.

Creating Opportunities

Addressing the sexuality needs of students with DD is far more complex than attempting to suppress sexual behavior, promoting basic hygiene, and protecting one's self from exploitation or abuse. Rather, special educators, related personnel, and parents must work together to promote appropriate sexual behavior and encourage various platonic and intimate relationships that are consistent with social norms. They must empower students to make decisions about their bodies, values, sexual and reproductive health, and role as sexual beings in a society that glamorizes sexuality while simultaneously treating it as a source of shame and embarrassment. In order to become fully self-determined, people with disabilities must be provided with the knowledge and skills to take care of themselves, protect themselves, and engage in meaningful sexual relationships to their fullest potential. The strategies reviewed here are by no means an exhaustive list. Although behavior-based strategies, social skills instruction, and video modeling can support student learning, there are numerous other teaching strategies that are effective for teaching students with DD. The intervention research literature specific to sex education for people with DD is extremely limited (Travers et al., in press), but this does not excuse educators from providing sex education throughout childhood and into adulthood. Rather, special educators should look to proven methods of instruction, a comprehensive sex education curriculum, and the unique needs of each student to achieve the best possible outcomes.

References

Alberto, P. A., & Troutman, A. C. (2009). *Applied behavior analysis for teachers* (8th ed.). Upper Saddle River, NJ: Merrill.

Bellini, S. (2008). *Building social relationships: A systematic approach to teaching social interaction skills to children and adolescents with autism spectrum disorders and other social difficulties.* Shawnee Mission, KS: AAPC.

Bernert, D. J. (2011). Sexuality and disability in the lives of women with intellectual disabilities. *Sexuality and Disability, 29,* 129–141. http://dx.doi.org/10.1007/s11195-010-9190-4

Blanchett, W. J., & Wolfe, P. S. (2002). A review of sex education curricula: Meeting the sex education needs of individuals with moderate and severe intellectual disabilities. *Research and Practice for Persons with Severe Disabilities, 27,* 43–57. http://dx.doi.org/10.2511/rpsd.27.1.43

Brekke, B. (1988). *Sexuality education for persons with severe developmental disabilities revised edition.* Santa Monica, CA: James Stanfield Publishing Co.

Cooper, J., Heron, T., & Heward, W. (2007). *Applied behavior analysis.* Upper Saddle River, NJ: Pearson Education.

Couwenhoven, T. (2007). *Teaching children with Down syndrome about their bodies, boundaries, and sexuality.* Bethesda, MD: Woodbine House.

Franzone, E. (2009). *Overview of task analysis.* Madison, WI: University of Wisconsin National Professional Development Center on Autism Spectrum Disorders and Waisman Center.

Franzone, E., & Collet-Klingenberg, L. (2008). *Overview of video modeling.* Madison, WI: University of Wisconsin National Professional Development Center on Autism Spectrum Disorders and Waisman Center.

Gray, C. A. (2000). *The new social story book.* Arlington, TX: Future Horizons.

Hingsburger, D. (2000). *Hand made love: A guide for teaching about male masturbation through understanding and video.* Ontario, Canada: Diverse City Press.

Hingsburger, D., & Haar, S. (2000). *Finger tips: Teaching women with disabilities about masturbation through understanding and video.* Ontario, Canada: Diverse City Press.

Hollomotz, A., & The Speakup Committee. (2008). "May we please have sex tonight?" People with learning difficulties pursuing privacy in residential group settings. *British Journal of Learning Disabilities, 37,* 91–97. http://dx.doi.org/10.1111/j.1468-3156.2008.00512.x

Kagohara, D. M., Achmadi, D., van der Meer, L., Lancioni, G. E., O'Reilly, M., Lang, R., … Sigafoos, J. (2013). Teaching two students with Asperger syndrome to greet adults using social stories and video modeling. *Journal of Developmental and Physical Disabilities, 25,* 241–251. http://dx.doi.org/10.1007/s10882-012-9300-6

Kempton, W. (2005). *Life horizons I & II.* Santa Barbara, CA: James Stanfield.

Klett, L. S., & Turan, Y. (2011). Generalized effects of social stories with task analysis for teaching menstrual care to three young women with autism. *Sexuality and Disability, 30,* 319–336. http://dx.doi.org/10.1007/s11195-011-9244-2

Koegel, L. K., Koegel, R. L., Frea, W., & Green-Hopkins, I. (2003). Priming as a method of coordinating educational services for students with autism. *Language, Speech, and Hearing Services in Schools, 34,* 228–235.

Konstantareas, M. M., & Lunsky, Y. L. (1997). Sociosexual knowledge, experience, attitudes, and interests of individuals with autistic disorder and developmental delay. *Journal of Autism and Developmental Disorders, 27,* 397–413.

Lesseliers, J., & Van Hove, G. (2002). Barriers to the development of intimate relationships and the expression of sexuality among people with developmental disabilities: Their perceptions. *Research and Practice for Persons with Severe Disabilities 27,* 69–81. http://dx.doi.org/10.2511/rpsd.27.1.69

Mansell, S., Sobsey, D., & Moskal, R. (1998). Clinical findings among sexually abused children with and without developmental disabilities. *Mental Retardation, 36,* 12–22. http://dx.doi.org/10.1352/0047-6765(1998)036<0012:cfasac>2.0.co;2

Mechling, L. C., & Ayres, K. M. (2012). A comparative study: Completion of fine motor office related tasks by high school students with autism using video models on large and small screen size. *Journal of Autism and Developmental Disorders, 42,* 2364-2375. http://dx.doi.org/10.1007/s10803-012-1484-1

National Commission on Adolescent Sexual Health. (1995). *Facing facts: Sexual health for America's adolescents.* New York, NY: Sexuality Information and Education Council of the United States.

Neitzel, J. (2010). *Response interruption/redirection for children and youth with autism spectrum disorders: Online training module.* Chapel Hill, NC: University of North Carolina National Professional Development Center on Autism Spectrum Disorders, FPG Child Development Institute.

Neitzel, J., & Wolery, M. (2009). *Overview of prompting.* Chapel Hill, NC: University of North Carolina National Professional Development Center on Autism Spectrum Disorders, FPG Child Development Institute.

Ohio Center for Autism and Low Incidence. (2013). *Autism internet modules.* Columbus, OH: Author. Available from www.autisminternetmodules.org.

Ray, F., Marks, C., & Bray-Garretson, H. (2004). Challenges to treating adolescents with Asperger's syndrome who are sexually abusive. *Sexual Addiction & Compulsivity, 11,* 265–285. http://dx.doi.org/10.1080/10720160490900614

Rosenberg, N. E., Schwartz, I. S., & Davis, C. A. (2010). Evaluating the utility of commercial videotapes for teaching hand washing to children with autism. *Education and Treatment of Children, 33,* 443–455. http://dx.doi.org/10.1353/etc.0.0098

Sansosti, F. J., Powell-Smith, K. A., & Kincaid, D. (2004). A research synthesis of social story interventions for children with autism spectrum disorders. *Focus on Autism and Other Developmental Disabilities, 19,* 194–204. http://dx.doi.org/10.1177/10883576040190040101

Schreibman, L., Whalen, C., & Stahmer, A. (2000). The use of video priming to reduce disruptive transition behavior in children with autism. *Journal of Positive Behavior Interventions, 2,* 3–11. http://dx.doi.org/10.1177/109830070000200102

Sexuality Information Education Center of the United States (SIECUS). (2004). *Guidelines for comprehensive sex education* (3rd ed.). Retrieved from www.siecus.org.

Shukla-Mehta, S., Miller, T., & Callahan, K. J. (2010). Evaluating the effectiveness of video instruction on social and communication skills for children with autism spectrum disorders: A review of the literature. *Focus on Autism and Other Developmental Disabilities, 25,* 23–36. http://dx.doi.org/10.1177/1088357609352901

Siperstein, G., & Paige, R., (2004). *Promoting social success: A curriculum for children with special needs.* Baltimore, MD: Brookes.

Stefanos, P., Maria, G., & Elias, K. (2011). Asperger syndrome and sexuality: Intervention issues in a case of an adolescent with Asperger syndrome in a context of a special educational setting. *Procedia Social and Behavioural Sciences, 15,* 490–495. http://dx.doi.org/10.1016/j.sbspro.2011.03.128

Stokes, M., & Kaur, A. (2005). High-functioning autism and sexuality: A parental perspective. *Autism, 9*, 266–289. http://dx.doi.org/10.1177/1362361305053258

Swango-Wilson, A. (2011). Meaningful sex education programs for individuals with intellectual/developmental disabilities. *Sexuality and Disability, 29*, 113–118. http://dx.doi.org/10.1007/s11195-010-9168-2

Sweeney, L. (2007). *Human sex education for students with special needs.* Shawnee Mission, KS: MarshMedia.

Tarnai, B., & Wolfe, P. S. (2008). Social stories for sex education for persons with autism/pervasive developmental disorder. *Sexuality and Disability, 26*, 29–36. http://dx.doi.org/10.1007/s11195-007-9067-3

Travers, J., & Tincani, M. (2010). Sex education for individuals with autism spectrum disorders: Critical issues and decision-making guidelines. *Education and Training in Autism and Developmental Disabilities, 45*, 284–293.

Travers, J., Tincani, M., Whitby, P. J. S., & Boutot, A. (in press). Alignment of sexuality education with self-determination for people with significant disabilities. *Education and Training in Autism and Developmental Disabilities.*

Travers, J., & Whitby, P. J. S. (in press). Sexuality and relationships. In M. Tincani & A. Bondy (Eds.), *Adults with autism spectrum disorder: Evidence-based and promising practices.* New York, NY: Guilford.

Walker-Hirsch, L. (2007). *Circles I: Intimacy and relationships.* Santa Barbara, CA: James Stanfield

Wehmeyer, M. L. (2001). Self-determination and mental retardation. In L. M. Glidden (Ed.), *International Review of Research in Mental Retardation,* (Vol. 24, pp. 1-4). San Diego, CA: Academic Press.

Wehmeyer, M. L., & Garner, N. W. (2003). The impact of personal characteristics of people with intellectual and developmental disability on self-determination and autonomous functioning. *Journal of Applied Research in Intellectual Disabilities, 16*, 255–265. http://dx.doi.org/10.1046/j.1468-3148.2003.00161.x

Wrobel, M. (2003). *Taking care of myself: A hygiene, puberty and personal curriculum for young people with autism.* Arlington, TX: Future Horizons.

Young Adult Institute. (2013). *The relationship series* [online videos]. Retrieved from www.yai.org

Zanolli, K., Daggett, J., & Adams, T. (1996). Teaching preschool autistic children to make spontaneous initiations to peers using priming. *Journal of Autism and Developmental Disorders, 26*, 407–422. http://dx.doi.org/10.1007/bf02172826